D0385215

THE OXFORD SCHOOL HARMONY COURSE

BOOK I

THE OXFORD SCHOOL HARMONY COURSE

BOOK I

BY

JAMES DENNY

West Riding Professor of Music
in the University of Leeds

LONDON
OXFORD UNIVERSITY PRESS
NEW YORK   TORONTO

Oxford University Press, Ely House, London W. 1

GLASGOW   NEW YORK   TORONTO   MELBOURNE   WELLINGTON
CAPE TOWN   SALISBURY   IBADAN   NAIROBI   DAR ES SALAAM   LUSAKA   ADDIS ABABA
BOMBAY   CALCUTTA   MADRAS   KARACHI   LAHORE   DACCA
KUALA LUMPUR   SINGAPORE   HONG KONG   TOKYO

ISBN 0 19 317202 X

First published 1960
Fifth impression 1971

Printed in Great Britain
by Lowe & Brydone (Printers) Limited, London, N.W.10

CONTENTS

INTRODUCTION

PART I—RUDIMENTS

Chapter   1   THE MAJOR SCALE   3

2   THE CLEFS   8

3   THE CHROMATIC SCALE   11

4   INTERVALS   16

5   TRIADS   23

6   THE MINOR SCALES   31

7   CADENCES   37

8   TIME AND ACCENT   43

PART II—INTRODUCTORY HARMONY

Chapter   9   THE PRINCIPLES OF PART-WRITING   53

10   TRIADS IN ROOT POSITION (MAJOR KEYS)   67

11   TRIADS IN THE FIRST INVERSION (MAJOR KEYS)   81

12   TWO-PART WRITING   88

13   UNACCENTED PASSING NOTES: UNACCENTED AUXILIARY NOTES: SUBSIDIARY HARMONY NOTES   96

14   TRIADS IN MINOR KEYS (ROOT POSITION AND FIRST INVERSION)   107

15   SUSPENSIONS   114

16   APPOGGIATURAS AND ACCIACCATURAS   126

17   TRIADS IN THE SECOND INVERSION   132

18   SIMPLE MODULATION IN FOUR PARTS   140

19   SIMPLE MODULATION IN TWO PARTS   153

20   THE CHORDS OF THE DOMINANT SEVENTH AND SUPERTONIC SEVENTH (ROOT POSITION)   158

21   THE DOMINANT SEVENTH AND SUPERTONIC SEVENTH (INVERSIONS)   168

22   ANTICIPATIONS: AND CONCLUSIONS   177

APPENDIX A.   MELODY-WRITING   183

APPENDIX B.   CONVENTIONS IN WRITING MUSIC MANUSCRIPT   195

INDEX OF QUOTATIONS   203

SUBJECT INDEX   207

v

INTRODUCTION

The Oxford School Harmony Course is intended as a text-book for those pupils who are preparing for public examinations, and for others who, unrestricted by an examination syllabus, wish to increase their knowledge and appreciation of music by theoretical study. For these reasons, the subject-matter of the principal chapters of this Course extends somewhat beyond the requirements of the General Certificate of Education. In addition, a quantity of material has been included which is complementary to the study of harmony, and helpful in promoting wider and more general musicianship. Thus, four topics touching on style and the pupil's mode of musical expression are discussed briefly in the appendices. Those on melody-writing and the conventions in writing music manuscript are printed in Book I: the two appendices in Book II refer to the problems of writing for strings and for the pianoforte. Further, a number of questions which might interrupt the main — thread of study are dealt with in a series of Notes in Book II. They are intended to satisfy, in some measure, the curiosity of enquiring pupils and to stimulate them to read more deeply in a dictionary or specialized text-book.

The Chapters in Part II—Introductory Harmony—will be generally regarded as having the most immediate value, since they bear directly on G.C.E. work. But it is hoped that the eight chapters in Part I will be helpful as guides to the revision of rudiments, or as foundations of a more thorough enquiry into the elements of musical theory.

Part III deals with the higher chords of the dominant and some common examples of chromatic harmony. These chapters (23-29) are short and lack the substance of a manual on Advanced Harmony. Yet pupils who are intending to study music after they have left school need some knowledge of these matters. Moreover, many such chords and progressions are within the experience of a sixth form musician and call for comment—even if the strict limits of his immediate syllabus are exceeded by so doing. The final chapters of Book II are devoted to J. S. Bach's harmonization of chorales and his keyboard Inventions. Not only do these subjects represent a logical culmination to the studies of an advanced pupil at school, but they are an important factor in the entrance tests to most universities.

The helpful practice of studying counterpoint at the same time as (and not after) chordal harmony has become more widespread of recent years. The present writer favours this step and has introduced a chapter on two-part writing early in Part II. Thereafter, exercises in two (as well as in four) parts are provided at the end of each succeeding chapter. No attempt has been made in Book I to explain the contrapuntal style of any particular period: it is more important for the pupil to learn to think horizontally while his confidence in harmonic thought and experiment is still incomplete. But in Book II more specific references are made to Morley and Bach; and others can be introduced by the teacher if circumstances are favourable.

Numerous quotations are given in both Books of this Course. It is hoped that they will whet the curiosity of the pupil, and perhaps prompt him to seek their sources. They demonstrate, in particular, the practice of the masters of the 17th and 18th centuries. There is some justification for this, for a knowledge of these classics remains the foundation of an understanding of the musical literature of all ages. An early awareness of the styles of Bach, Mozart and Beethoven in no way hinders a student as he becomes familiar with the music of other composers, other nationalities, and other centuries.

Roman numerals are used throughout this Course to indicate the root origin of chords. The positions of chords are described by the traditional figured bass. It is believed that the combination of these two systems is the most helpful ' shorthand ' for the beginner. But root numerals can outlive their usefulness. Pupils should be persuaded to omit them as soon as possible in their written work, and to rely on hearing the root progression in the mind's ear. Figured bass can then be used alone according to custom.

The exercises at the end of the chapters in Parts II and III are framed on the assumption that they will be worked on paper. But many can be made the basis of practical harmony at the keyboard if circumstances permit. Other tests appear in Book I: thus, some short passages are provided for class singing, to help pupils to hear the movement of vocal parts (and especially the bass). These are printed for soprano and alto, but they can also be sung by broken voices, or be transposed into more convenient keys. Those without words should be vocalized on a suitable vowel. The brief aural and keyboard tests in the earlier chapters can be extended at will. Exercises for unprepared dictation or aural training, based on the lessons learned in chapters 10–21, are printed in Book II. The use of C clefs may be introduced at any point at the discretion of the teacher.

To the Pupil

So soon as you begin to work musical exercises on paper or at the keyboard you are a composer. That should never be forgotten. Few of us become famous composers; yet many people, by a study of harmony, learn to write music which sounds well. The ear is the judge of the effect and merit of what we produce.

Do not wait until you are fully skilled in harmony and counterpoint before writing down musical ideas of your own. You should compose as much, and as soon, as possible. We all have ideas floating in our minds; yet it takes practice and effort to grasp them and transfer them to paper. The freedom of style in your own compositions will help you in working your harmony exercises: the reverse is also true. But whatever you write, it should be musical; and however simple it may be, it should be judged as a work of art.

In this book, many of the illustrations are taken from the works of the great masters. Look at them carefully; play them on the piano. By doing so you will gradually build up an awareness of musical style. Your eye will help your ear to hear these quotations as you look at them. Try hard to cultivate co-operation between eye and ear. As an incentive to you in this matter, the special features which the examples and quotations are intended to illustrate are frequently left unmarked: you must search for them yourself.

ACKNOWLEDGEMENTS

Acknowledgements are due to the following for permission to quote extracts from the works listed: Boosey & Hawkes Ltd. (Béla Bartók, *Mikrokosmos*, and C. V. Stanford, ' Devon, O Devon ' from *Songs of the Sea*); Curwen Edition (Gustav Holst, *The Planets*); Durand & Cie (Claude Debussy, String Quartet and *Pelléas et Mélisande*, and Camille Saint-Saëns, *Danse Macabre*); Editions Jean Jobert (Claude Debussy, *Prélude à l'après-midi d'un faune*); Oxford University Press. (R. Vaughan Williams, *Job*, and William Walton, *Belshazzar's Feast*); Stainer & Bell Ltd. (Gustav Holst, ' Funeral Hymn ' from the *Rig Veda*, C. V. Stanford, ' Sailing at Dawn ' from *Songs of the Fleet*, and R. Vaughan Williams, ' Just as the Tide was Flowing ' from *Five English Folk Songs*).

PART I
RUDIMENTS

I. THE MAJOR SCALE

Tonality

1. Almost all music written and performed in Europe, the American continent, and wherever Western influences are felt, is governed by a relationship between melody and harmony which is described as Tonality, or Key.

2. Tonality itself is founded on a series of notes called a Scale.[1] There are two forms of scale to each key—a major and a minor scale. Only the major scale is considered in this chapter. The minor scale is discussed in Chapter 6.

The Major Scale

3. You may be familiar with the major scale in sol-fa terms—*doh, ray, me, fah, soh, lah, te, doh¹*. You will remember that *doh* is the key-note, the foundation of the tonality of a particular key. The other names follow upwards in sequence.

Degree Names

4. But there are other (and more usual) names for the degrees of the scale. These help to explain the place and duty of each degree in the scale. Read the following table upwards from the bottom—and compare it with Fig. 1.

I   *Tonic*—the key-note.

VII *Leading note*—one degree below the tonic: the note which often leads up to the tonic.

VI   *Submediant*—midway between the tonic and the subdominant when descending: that is, three degrees *below* the tonic.

V   *Dominant*—five degrees above the tonic: the most important note of the scale after the tonic.

IV   *Subdominant*—think of this *either* as one degree below the dominant (V) *or* as five degrees below the tonic.

III *Mediant*—midway between the tonic and the dominant: an important note in distinguishing between major and minor tonality.

II   *Supertonic*—one degree above the tonic.

I   *Tonic*—the key-note: the foundation of the tonality of the scale.

[1] See also Note in Book II.

3

Fig. 1

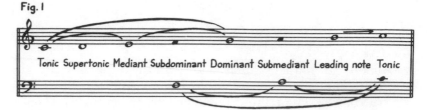

Tonic Supertonic Mediant Subdominant Dominant Submediant Leading note Tonic

5. It may be convenient to use sol-fa names occasionally (as when singing a succession of notes); but the degree-names given in para. 4 are in general use amongst musicians: they should be memorized.

6. Most of us are familiar with the look of the pianoforte keyboard. But for ease of reference here is a diagram of a portion of one.

Fig. 2

C D E F G A BC D E F G A B C D E

7. The degree-names in Fig. 1 are set against a scale beginning and ending on C. It will be seen from Fig. 2 that this scale uses only white notes. Listen while these notes are played on the piano. They are a major scale: and since the first note (the tonic) is C, the scale is said to be that of C major.

Intervals in the Major Scale

8. The interval between one note and the next, black or v.hite, on the piano keyboard is one semitone. Two semitones make up one tone.

9. A comparison of Figs. 1 and 2 shows that some degrees of a major scale are one tone, and some one semitone apart.

B—C	(leading note—tonic)	Semitone
A—B	(submed.—leading note)	Tone
G—A	(dom.—submed.)	Tone
F—G	(subdom.—dom.)	Tone
E—F	(mediant—subdom.)	Semitone
D—E	(supertonic—mediant)	Tone
C—D	(tonic—supertonic)	Tone

10. The order of tones and semitones in a major scale—every major scale—is, therefore, T T S T T T S.

11. A scale can begin on any note. But if it is to be a major scale,

and have that note as the tonic, it must be built in the order
T T S T T T S.

Fig. 3

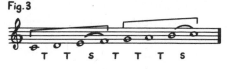

T T S T T T S

Tetrachords

12. Fig. 3 shows that a major scale is composed of two groups of
four notes, each spaced T T S, and that these groups lie a tone
apart: T T S – T – T T S. These two groups are called Tetrachords. ('Tetrachord', a Greek word, was the name given to the
four notes of the ancient lyre which covered the interval of a
perfect fourth. The modern tetrachord to which we are now
referring also extends over a perfect fourth.)

13. If a major scale is composed of two tetrachords set a tone
apart, one can form a new major scale by beginning with the
upper tetrachord (of the original scale) and proceeding upwards;
and also form another major scale by beginning with the *lower*
tetrachord and proceeding downwards.

Fig. 4

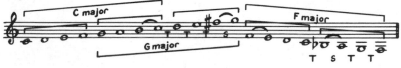

14. It will be seen from Fig. 4 that if you begin with the upper
tetrachord of C major (on G, the dominant of C) and add
another tetrachord above it, one note must be raised a semitone
in order to get the correct sequence of tones and semitones. The
major scale of the dominant of C, therefore, requires a key-signature of one sharp (F sharp), whereas the scale of C major has
neither sharp nor flat.

15. Similarly, if you play the lower tetrachord of C downwards
(that is, beginning on F, the subdominant) the first note of the
additional tetrachord must begin on B *flat* (not B natural) in order
that the two tetrachords shall be one tone apart. So the major
scale of the subdominant of C requires a key-signature of one flat
(B flat).

Exercises

1. Play on the piano a major scale *upwards*, beginning on C. Then
form a second scale on the dominant of C (the first note of the
upper tetrachord). After this, begin a third scale on the dominant

of the second scale: note the name of the key and the number and names of the sharpened notes necessary to maintain the order of T T S T T T S.

2. Begin on C and play a major scale downwards. Then form a second scale on the subdominant of C (the first note of the lower tetrachord). Continue to add tetrachords (downwards) and note the name of each key and the number and names of the flattened notes necessary to maintain the correct order of tones and semitones.

The Cycle of Major Keys

16. The experiment in Exercises 1 and 2 should show that, beginning with the scale of C major, sharps are increased by beginning a fresh major scale on the dominant of the previous key: that is, a fifth higher. Flats are increased by beginning a fresh scale on the subdominant of the previous key: a fifth lower.

17. But if we continue upwards (or downwards) in the manner described we return in due course to our original key. Thus:

Fig. 5

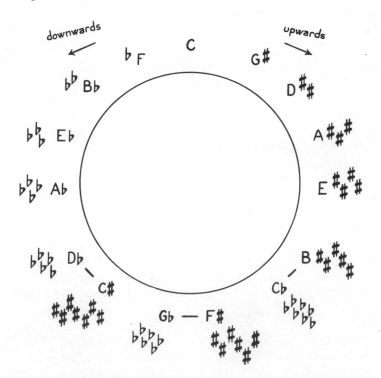

18. Where the upward and downward progressions meet in Fig. 5 the scales are each given two descriptions. For F♯ can equally well be described as G♭ (so far as the notes on the piano are concerned): and C♭ can be renamed B. So if, after moving through the keys of A flat and D flat to G flat, the notes of the scale of G flat are renamed as those of the scale of F sharp, these notes are said to have undergone an enharmonic change: the sounds will be the same on the piano but they are given different names.

The Key-Signatures of Major Scales

19. While C major has neither sharp nor flat, we now know that G major has one sharp: F♯. This sharp is a semitone below the tonic. D major has two sharps: F♯ and (a semitone below D) C♯. 20. Sharps in major scales are added, therefore, by fifths upwards (or by fourths downwards): and the last sharp is always a semitone below the key-note:

Fig.6

C   G   D   A   E   B   F♯   C♯

21. From Fig. 5 it will be seen that F major has one flat: B flat. If, now, the lower tetrachord of F major is played downwards and another added to complete a scale of B flat, a second flat is necessary to ensure the correct order of tones and semitones: B♭ and E♭. 22. This shows that flats, in major scales, are added by fifths downwards (or by fourths upwards):

Fig.7

C   F   B♭   E♭   A♭   D♭   G♭   C♭

The recognition of Key from the Key-signature

23. A major key can be found from its signature *either* by naming the note a semitone higher than the last sharp: *or* by naming the last flat *but one*. Thus, B flat major has two flats: B♭ and E♭. And D flat has five, of which the last but one is D♭. (An exception is F major which has only one flat.)

B

Fig. 8

D major   B major   E♭ major   D♭ major

Exercises

3. Write down the degree names of the notes named (by the teacher) in the scales of C, G, and F major.

4. Write down the interval—tone or semitone—between named notes in the scales of C, A, B♭ major.

5. What new scale is formed from the upper tetrachord of D, B, C and F♯ major? Write down the key-signatures of these new scales in the treble clef.

6. What new scale is formed from the lower tetrachord of F, A♭, G♭ and E♭ major? Write down the key-signatures of these new scales in the treble clef.

7. How can a major key be identified from its key-signature? Give the major key to which the following signatures belong.

Ex. 7

8. Play on the piano upwards, then downwards, the scales of G, B♭, A and D♭ major.

9. Write down the notes which, in a named key, are (*i*) the submediant; (*ii*) the supertonic; (*iii*) the subdominant; (*iv*) the mediant; (*v*) the dominant of the tonic.

2. THE CLEFS

1. Musical notation includes the groups and lines of spaces called staves which are used to indicate pitch. They were first used in a system developed and popularized (if not invented) by a Benedictine monk named Guido d'Arezzo in the eleventh century.

2. By this system, a series of six-note scales or *hexachords* was built up from a fundamental note (corresponding to our bottom G in the bass clef) which was placed on the lowest line of all. (A full explanation of this system is out of place in this book, but will be found in any musical dictionary in articles on ' Guido d'Arezzo ' or ' Gamut '.) The following table shows how the seven hexachords, each set out in the order T T S T T, produced a succession

of notes extending from (our modern) bass G to treble E by means of eleven lines and the intervening spaces. (As B♭ as well as B♮ was recognized, it was possible to build the hexachords beginning on F.)

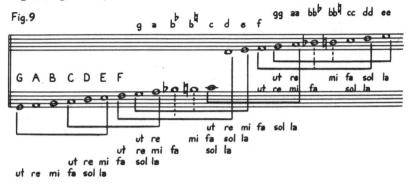

Fig. 9

3. The degrees of each hexachord were named Ut, Re, Mi, Fa, Sol, La—thus anticipating the modern sol-fa system by nearly 900 years.

4. The grid of eleven lines is sometimes referred to in text-books as the Great Stave. It had no such name at the time of the development of the Guidonian System. Manuscripts exist from this period which show that the number of lines used might vary from four to more than eleven. For instance, it became the custom for ecclesiastical plainsong to be written on a stave of only four lines. But however many lines were bracketed in a stave, a mark was always made to show where C, F or G were placed, according to the needs of the music.

5. As choral (and instrumental) music developed and began to extend over a wider range of the Guidonian System, so it became customary to select the most convenient *five* lines of the eleven, marking 'middle' C, F, or G as the case might be. Our present-day treble stave is in reality the top five lines of this system: our bass stave is the bottom five: while ' middle ' C is a leger line between the two staves.

6. In addition, there are (four) other groups of five-line staves all of which have a clef-sign marking the line belonging to ' middle ' C. These have come to be known as C clefs, though each has also its own name (Fig. 10).

7. The following diagram shows the position of the C, F and G clefs in relation to ' middle ' C.

Fig. 10

8. Learn the G and F clefs at once. And develop a familiarity with the alto and tenor clefs before studying Book II, as both these are used in writing for strings.

9. Notes placed on five-line staves are said to be simpler to read than if they were laid on a grid of eleven lines. On the other hand, reading from an unfamiliar clef is confusing at first. Regular practice is needed to make the recognition of notes instantaneous. Learn the positions of C, F, and G in a new clef: thereafter other notes will spring to the eye and the complete series will gradually be mastered.

10. Full details of clefs used by orchestral instruments can be found in a dictionary or treatise on orchestration. Here is a summary of the voices and instruments which regularly, or occasionally, use the four chief clefs.

Treble (*G*):   treble or soprano voice; all treble woodwind; french
                   horn; trumpet; violin.
Alto: alto voice (old scores); alto trombone; viola.
Tenor: tenor voice (old scores); bassoon; tenor trombone;
                   cello
Bass (*F*):   bass voice; bassoon; bass trombone; tuba; cello and
                   double-bass.

11. In music for four voices on two staves, the tenor part shares a stave with the bass part (Figs. 105, 114, etc.). But when the tenor is given a separate stave, the *treble clef* is generally used and the part is written an octave higher than it sounds. If confusion is likely to arise (with the soprano and alto parts in the treble clef), a figure 8 is placed below, or a small letter C at the side of, the clef sign (Figs. 115 and 116) as a reminder that the notes sound an octave lower than written.

12. When the parts for several voices or instruments are written on two staves, they are said to be in ' short score ' (Figs. 94, 107,

etc.). When each voice or instrument has a stave to itself, the
writing is said to be in ' open score ' (Figs. 115 and 116).
Exercises

1. Write down two examples of the following notes in each of
the four chief clefs (treble, alto, tenor and bass): C, G and F:
F♯, C♯, B♭ and E♭.

2. Write down in a named clef a series of notes dictated alpha-
betically. (Simple dictation in a named clef may also be given
from the piano.)

3. Play on the piano the following phrases in a named clef.

Ex. 3 (i)

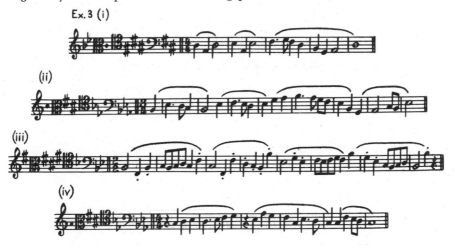

4. Transpose, on paper, a given melody from the treble to the
alto clef: and a given melody from bass to tenor clef.

3. THE CHROMATIC SCALE

1. This chapter is introduced at this point to explain the meaning
in music of two important terms—diatonic and chromatic.
(Paras. 7–19 need not be studied until after reading Chapter 6.)

2. A major scale is said to be diatonic because all its notes belong
to the key of the tonic. For the same reason, a piece of music is
said to be diatonic if it only uses notes belonging to the scale of the
key in which it is written. Thus, the melodies of ' Drink to me only

with thine eyes ' and ' Auld Lang Syne ' are diatonic since no note
in either is foreign to the scale of the tonic key.

3. When the minor scales are considered in Chapter 6, it will be
found that the term diatonic can equally well be applied to music
using only the notes of the minor scales.   In this case *some* accidentals [1] may have to be used (as when the leading note is sharpened at a cadence).   Yet the melody does not necessarily cease
to be diatonic because of this.   In ' Charlie is my darling ' we
find two accidentals because, to write in the melodic minor, the
sixth and seventh degrees of the scale may have to be raised a
semitone (see Chapters 6, para. 9).

Fig. 11 (Key: Cmin.)

This melody, therefore, is also diatonic in spite of its accidentals.

4. But if we compare the phrase in Fig. 12 with the more elaborate
version from Chopin's Nocturne in G major (Fig. 13) we find that
two notes are introduced—C♯ and A♯—which do not belong to
G major. These two notes are chromatic.

Fig. 12 (Key: Gmaj.)   Fig. 13   Chopin
                              Andante

5. Again, the opening of the Nocturne in E♭ has the following
diatonic melody:

Fig. 14 (Key: E♭)

Later, this simple phrase is ornamented (Fig. 15) by the addition

---

[1] An accidental is a sign (sharp, double sharp, flat, double flat, or natural) which
temporarily raises or lowers a note in contradiction of the key-signature. The sign
holds good for the duration of the bar in which it is written, unless cancelled by a
further accidental.

of extra notes; some diatonic and others (A♮, C♭ and C♯) chromatic. The chromatic notes do not belong to the prevailing key of E♭ major.

Fig. 15   Chopin

6. This book is chiefly concerned with diatonic harmony. But examples of chromaticism are so common that we cannot ignore their existence, even in the early stages of our studies. Take careful note, therefore, of any accidentals which appear in exercises or examples. Analyse them to test if they are chromatic or diatonic. (See also Chapters 6 and 14).

*   *   *   *

The Chromatic Scale

7. Just as it is possible to play a sequence of notes which, by the arrangement of its intervals, can be termed a major or minor scale, so it is possible to sound a scale using consecutively all twelve notes of the octave. But in doing so several notes will be included which belong neither to the major nor to the minor scales of the initial note.—For instance, if we begin on C and play upwards all the notes in the octave, the note between C and D, and that between F and G, do not belong to C major or C minor. Such notes will be chromatic.

8. A scale containing all the semitones is termed a chromatic scale.

9. Let us assume, in writing a chromatic scale, we are to begin on C. We take the harmonic form of the scale of C minor (not C major) as a basis and borrow accidentals from the keys nearly related to C minor.

10. The keys relative to C minor are:
    F minor
    G minor
    E♭ major
    A♭ major
    B♭ major

11. The semitone above C will be D♭ (taken from F minor and A♭ major): there is no C♯ in any of the related keys. After D♮ there will follow E♭: D♯ is not contained in any related key. But after F♮ there will be F♯ (the leading note of G minor), not G♭. And we shall have B♭ as there is no A♯.

12. The completed scale, known as the harmonic chromatic scale, will then read:

Fig. 16

13. In Fig. 16 two notes remain untouched by accidentals, the 'tonic' and the 'dominant'. So the scale consists of the following intervals from the tonic:

Major and Minor	2nd, 3rd, 6th, 7th
Perfect and Augmented	4th
Perfect	5th (and 8ve.)

14. Remember the principles upon which the accidentals are chosen: they will help to clarify problems arising in Book II from modulations and from the use of chromatic chords. For the moment it is sufficient to remember that the harmonic chromatic scale accounts for the following passage being written as it is:

Fig. 17 (Key: Cmaj.)

and not

15. Sometimes chromatic scales are written:

Fig. 18

This system reduces the number of accidentals and is easier to read. It is the melodic chromatic scale. Sharps are used in ascending, and flats in descending. Note that neither the 'tonic' nor the 'dominant' are free from accidentals as they are in the harmonic form of this scale.

16. Chromatic passages in compositions are often a mixture of semitones with larger intervals. Such is the case in the opening bars of Debussy's *Prélude à l'après-midi d'un faune*.

Fig.19   Debussy

Exercise

1. Rewrite the following, adding the signature to the appropriate major key and leaving out the accidentals before all the notes which are diatonic.

4. INTERVALS

Definition

1. A musical interval is the difference in pitch between two notes sounded simultaneously or consecutively. Two notes played simultaneously form an harmonic interval: played consecutively they form a melodic interval.

Keyboard Intervals

2. The interval between any two adjacent notes on the piano keyboard is one semitone. Two semitones make up one tone. This confirms what was learned in Chapter 1: that the intervals from C to D and from D to E are both one tone—each being separated by one note: and that the interval from E to F is a semitone, since these two notes are adjacent.

Diatonic and Chromatic Semitones

3. A semitone described with different alphabetical letters is a diatonic semitone. That using the same letter is a chromatic semitone.

Fig.20

Diatonic Semitones   Chromatic Semitones

Reckoning of Intervals

4. Intervals are reckoned and named by counting the degrees of the diatonic scale. Just as there is only one note on each space or line of the stave in a diatonic scale so, in reckoning intervals, only one note is counted on each space or line. The extreme notes of an interval are *both* counted.

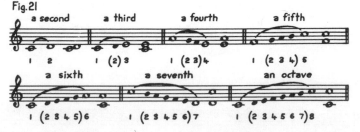

Fig.21

a second   a third   a fourth   a fifth

1   2   1 (2)3   1 (2 3)4   1 (2 3 4) 5

a sixth   a seventh   an octave

1 (2 3 4 5)6   1 (2 3 4 5 6)7   1 (2 3 4 5 6 7)8

5. Fig. 21 shows that intervals can be reckoned upwards or downwards. (The unison, when two or more parts sound the same note, is omitted since it cannot be termed a chord.)

Types of Interval

6. Of the intervals which exist between the notes of a major scale and its *lower* tonic, some are said to be perfect and others major:

Fig 22

7. If a perfect interval is made less by one *chromatic* semitone it is said to be diminished. A major interval reduced by a *chromatic* semitone becomes minor: a minor interval so reduced is said to be diminished.

Fig. 23

8. If a perfect interval is enlarged by one *chromatic* semitone it is said to be augmented. A minor interval so enlarged becomes major; and a major interval, augmented.

Fig. 24

9. Study Figs. 22, 23 and 24. While it is possible to reckon intervals by counting the semitones they contain, it is clumsy and may lead

to some wrong answers. For instance, reference to the piano will suggest that E♭ to F and D♯ to F are equal intervals since the same notes are depressed in each case. But as any kind of E and any kind of F lie on an adjacent line and space the interval between them must be some form of *second*. On the other hand, the interval between any kind of D and any kind of F must be some form of *third* since the two notes lie on adjacent spaces separated by a line. The exact form of the second or the third can be reckoned by the presence or absence of accidentals.

Fig.25

In the instances quoted, E♭ to F is a major second; and D♯ to F is a diminished third.

10. To reckon any interval, begin by deciding *what kind* of interval it can be (a third, fifth, etc.): then, assuming the lower note to be the tonic of a major key, take any accidentals into account and decide the *nature* of the interval (major, perfect, minor, etc.).

Fig.26

Compound Intervals

11. Intervals which are more than an octave are called compound. An octave and a third make a tenth (*not* an eleventh).

8ve + 5th = 12th
8ve + 8ve (two octaves) = 15th

12. Compound intervals are usually referred to in terms of the simple interval. An exception, in ' figuring ' a bass, is the ninth which is frequently written as 9 (Fig. 197).

Inversion of Intervals

13. If the lower note of an interval is transposed an octave higher, that interval is said to have been inverted. An octave becomes a unison: a seventh, a second: a sixth, a third: a fifth, a fourth: and vice versa.

14. At the inversion, a major interval becomes minor: a diminished interval becomes augmented: and vice versa. But a perfect interval remains perfect.

Fig. 27

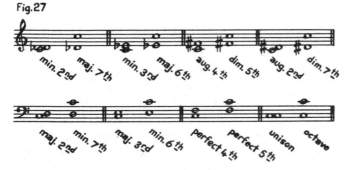

The Quality of Intervals

15. The quality or character of individual intervals is connected with the question of concord and discord.

16. The distinction between concord and discord is unaffected by the form of the interval. Some perfect, major and minor intervals are consonant, others are dissonant: and the same may be said of augmented and diminished intervals. The distinction is based on the judgement of the ear: fashion also plays no small part in deciding these matters. Throughout the centuries opinion has varied widely as to what the ear considers to be discordant. There have also been subtle distinctions between the degrees of ' perfection ' of two concords. It can be argued that to the modern ear many traditional discords have lost their harshness and are rapidly being accepted as concords. But for the purposes of this study of harmony, the practice of the great composers from about 1600 to the early years of the present century will be regarded as the accepted standard.

17. The concordant intervals are:

        .the (perfect) octave
        the perfect fifth
        the major and minor sixths
        the major and minor thirds

Of these, the octave and the fifth were regarded (up to about 1500) as ' perfect ' concords: the sixths and thirds as ' imperfect ' concords.

18. The discords are:

> the major and minor sevenths
> the major and minor seconds
> the perfect fourth
> and (for the present) all augmented and diminished intervals

The Perfect Fourth

19. Reference to the perfect fourth as a discord calls for some comment. In the early period of part-writing (10th–12th centuries) this interval was regarded, with the octave and the perfect fifth, as a concord of the greatest ' perfection '. By the 14th century it had fallen from grace and was relegated to the category of discords. Almost simultaneously with this great change, the third was promoted from a position of bare tolerance to one of imperfect consonance. Such may be the changes of aesthetic fashion: the ear is, finally, the judge of what sounds satisfactory or unsatisfactory.

20. In our present studies, the perfect fourth when lying between two upper parts is without doubt concordant, whether sounded as an harmonic or a melodic interval.

21. In neither of the above examples is the presence of a fourth offensive to the ear. All these chords are consonant. This is because the bass notes emphasize that each chord is made up of a third and a sixth (from the bass), both of which are consonant intervals.

22. But the sounding of a fourth *from the bass* is a different matter. Wagner realized this when, in his opera *The Mastersingers of Nuremberg*, he writes the following passage for Beckmesser to play

on the lute. The effect is stark, odd, and ludicrous—which is
what Wagner intended.

Fig.30   Wagner
Moderato

Fig. 31
(i)   (ii)   (iii)   (iv)

23. Study the interval of a perfect fourth carefully. Listen to
example (*i*) in Fig. 31. Your own ear must decide the quality of
this sound. You will not, perhaps, regard it as harsh or rough (for
discords are not necessarily ugly), but as having a bare, tense
quality which possesses little sense of repose. The chord at (*ii*)
will probably appear less bare, due to the softening effect of the
sixth: but there is no greater feeling of finality. At (*iii*) and (*iv*)
are two progressions which can remedy this unstable effect. The
tension of the fourth at (*iii*) is exchanged for the clarity and perfection of the fifth: but it is only an exchange and not a true
resolution. At (*iv*), on the other hand, the *fall* of the fourth above
the bass to the third gives relief to the existing tension. This is the
progression which has proved, throughout some five centuries, to
be an ideal resolution to the discordant interval of a fourth from
the bass (Chap. 5, paras. 26 and 27).

24. The Note on Forbidden Consecutives in Book II refers to
phrases in which fourths predominate. While such passages are
not our immediate concern the following example, dating from
the 9th century, should be played or sung. It is a short example
of what is called Organum. It illustrates the quality of the fourth.
The two parts spring from a unison and proceed in a series of
consecutive fourths before joining together to form the cadence or
close. By singing it or playing it on the piano you can, perhaps,
understand better the two opposite points of view : the early
acceptance of the fourth as a concord, and (from about the 14th
century) its classification as a discord.

Fig. 32

Rex coe-li Do-mi-ne ma - ris un - di- so-ni:
Ty - ta - nis ni- ti- di   squa- li - di - que so- li.

25. Before concluding this chapter we may well consider the structure of the octave and the intervals it contains. Much of the character and variety of western music is due to the way they are arranged. This arrangement, in its turn, is governed to a large extent by the order of tones and semitones in the major and minor scales. While the octave groups (of 13 notes) are the same up and down the piano, differing only in pitch, their contents are complex. The dominant, for instance, is not placed centrally but eight-thirteenths of the distance between the tonic and its upper octave. Variety and ' unbalance ' are also to be found on inverting intervals. Yet though the internal structure of the octave may be confusing at first, composers of many centuries have found its very lack of symmetry a rich source of opportunity.

Exercises

1. Sing the following exercises as studies in pitching tones and semitones.

Ex.1
(i)

(ii)

(iii)

2. Sing, write down, or play on the piano the following intervals from a given note. (Treble and bass clefs only should be used for written dictation in the first instance.)

perfect 5th: minor 3rd: major 2nd: major 7th:
minor 7th: major 3rd: minor 6th: perfect 4th:
major 6th.

3. Name the following intervals.

Ex.3
(i)

(ii)

4. Write down the inversion of named intervals.

5. TRIADS

Definition

1. A triad is a chord composed of three sounds: a root; a note a fifth above the root; and a note a third above the root.

2. If the fifth is perfect, a triad containing a major third is termed a major triad; and one with a minor third, a minor triad. These are sometimes referred to as Common Chords.

3. If the fifth is diminished (and the third minor), the triad is said to be diminished. If the fifth is augmented (and the third major), the triad is said to be augmented.

Fig. 33

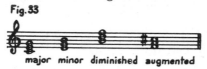

major   minor   diminished   augmented

Root Position

4. A triad whose root is the lowest note sounded is in its root position.

5. It is possible to form a triad on every degree of the scale. In C major the available triads in root position are:

Fig. 34

C I   II   III   IV   V   VI   VII

6. For convenience, triads in root position can be indicated by the (Roman) number of the degree of the scale on which the root stands (Chap. 1, para. 4). The Roman numeral will stand by itself unless there is a special reason for referring to the third or the fifth; as (for instance) when the third is to be raised or lowered a semitone by an accidental.—II♯, V♭.

7. If it is necessary to indicate the key in which the Roman numerals stand, a capital letter will show that it is major, and a small letter that it is minor (Figs, 34, 39 and 47).

c

8. It will be seen in Fig. 34 that the triad on the leading note, VII, contains a diminished fifth and is therefore dissonant. Its use and treatment will be discussed in Chapters 19 and 20, and for the present it is sufficient to mention that, on quitting it, the leading note will generally rise and the subdominant fall by step: the movement of the third is more variable.

9. The remaining triads in Fig. 34 contain a perfect fifth and are, on this account, consonant.

Primary Triads

10. The triads I, IV, and V are major, as the third from the root is major. They are called the primary triads of the key to which they belong. Standing on the tonic, subdominant, and dominant respectively, they are the chords which establish the key most strongly.

Secondary Triads

11. II, III, and VI, containing a minor third, are minor triads: they are the secondary triads of the key to which they belong. (Chapter 10, para. 19.)

Spacing

12. A triad is recognized as such even though one or both of the upper notes are converted into compound intervals. The following are different arrangements of the same triad in its root position. Note that the figuring is the same whether the intervals are simple or compound.

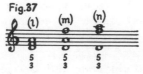

13. In Fig. 37, (l) is said to be in ' close ' position: (m) and (n) are in ' extended ' positions.

Exercises
1. Describe the following triads when they are played on the piano.

Ex. I

2. Write down on a single stave the primary triads of the following major keys: G, B♭, E, D♭, A, E♭.
3. Write down on a single stave the secondary triads of the following major keys: C, D, F, A♭, B, E♭.

Inversions
14. If the bottom note (the root) of a triad be raised an octave, the third becomes the bass of the chord and the upper notes will be a sixth and a third from the bass. This is called the first inversion (of the triad) or the chord of the sixth: it is figured ⁶₃ or, more often, **⁶**.[1] The *original bass* remains the root of the chord.
15. Similarly, if both the bottom note and the third of a triad in root position be raised above the fifth, the chord then becomes the second inversion (of the triad). The figuring will be ⁶₄, as the upper notes will be a sixth and a fourth above the bass. The *original bass* of the triad remains the root.

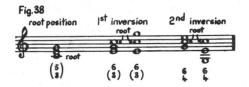

Fig. 38

16. The root of all the chords in Fig. 38 is C.
17. Remember that the root position, 1st inversion and 2nd inversion of the same triad are not *one chord*: they are *three* chords, each with its own colour and function. Listen carefully to these three different chords and learn to distinguish between them.

Exercises
4. Give the position of the following chords on hearing them sounded on the piano.

[1]See Note on Figured Bass in Book II.

Ex.4

5. Listen while the following phrases are played.
Give the position of each broken chord: then sing the phrases.

Ex.5

First Inversions

18. The following are the first inversions of triads in the scale of
C major. Note that the Roman numerals have the figure ^{6} added.

Fig.39

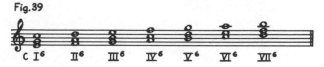

19. All the chords in Fig. 39 are consonant.

20. Though VII is dissonant in its root position because of the
diminished fifth above the bass, its first inversion is consonant.
Just as in VII, so in VII ^{6} the leading note usually rises and the
subdominant falls by step: the supertonic is, again, more free but
frequently falls to the tonic.

Fig.40

21. Learn to recognize the sound of any diatonic first inversion
in both an extended and the close position. In Fig. 41, (l), (n),

and (q) are in extended position: (m), (o), and (p) in close position.

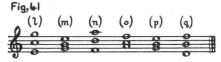

Fig. 41
(l) (m) (n) (o) (p) (q)

22. Reference will sometimes be made to the first (or second) inversion *of* C. This means the inversion of the triad whose root is C (as at (l) and (m) below).

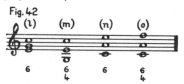

Fig. 42
(l)   (m)   (n)   (o)

6   6   6   6
         4   4

23. But a distinction must be made between an inversion *of* C and an inversion *on* C. The latter means an inversion whose bass note is sounding C (as at (n) and (o) above). The chord at (n) stands *on* C but is the first inversion *of* the triad of A minor, with root A. That at (o) is the second inversion *of* the triad of F major (root F), though it stands *on* C.

Exercise

6. Give the position of the following chords on hearing them played: state if they are major or minor. (The diminished triad belongs to both).

Ex. 6

Second Inversions

24. The following are the second inversions of triads in the scale of C major. The Roman numerals have the figures $\frac{6}{4}$ added:

Fig. 43

C I⁶₄ II⁶₄ III⁶₄ IV⁶₄ V⁶₄ VI⁶₄ VII⁶₄

25. Since the second inversion of the triad sounds a note a fourth above the bass, this chord will be treated as a discord. The six-four chord has a character and colour of its own and calls for special consideration. It will be discussed in Chapter 17; but one of its most common uses, in cadences, can be mentioned at once. In such cases the second inversion *of* the tonic is sounded *on* the dominant: then (in its simplest form) the dissonant fourth resolves on to the third of the dominant and the sixth on to the fifth, thereby completing the dominant triad: if the cadence is to be completed, this dominant triad (V) moves to the root position of the tonic (I) (Figs. 44 and 45).

Fig. 44

Fig. 45

26. A characteristic of the six-four chord is the impression it gives of being incomplete, of leaving a phrase unfinished. The 4 seems compelled to fall to 3 and (because of this) the 6 to 5. Learn to identify the sound of the six-four, and to ' feel ' the usual resolution.

Fig. 46

27. A memorable example of a six-four remaining unresolved is to be found at the end of the *allegretto* movement of Beethoven's 7th Symphony (Fig. 48). The tonic bass carried in the listener's mind from the last bar of the strings does nothing to dispel the magical effect of the wind sustaining this insecure discord. The movement had begun (Fig. 49) as it ended, but here the second inversion was replaced by the entry of the strings on the root position of the same chord.

28. Movement from one position of a chord to another is a common feature in music. The individual colour of the inversions of the triad is largely lost by reason of the impression that the tonic can be heard continuously in the bass: that is, in passages in which the inversions of the same chord succeed one another rapidly, the root impresses itself on the ear of the listener even when it is not being sounded.

Exercises

7. Describe the following chords when they are played on the piano. Give the position of the chords and state if they are major or minor.

Ex.7

8. Write down in the treble clef from dictation all the notes in the following chords. Name and figure the position of each chord.

Ex.8

9. Sing the following exercise, listening carefully to the colour and quality of each chord.

Ex.9

ye his | name with | one ac -cord, | one ac -cord; | Praise | the | Lord!

6. THE MINOR SCALES

1. A major scale is sounded when the white keys of the piano are played consecutively from C to C (Chap. 1).

2. In like manner, the minor scale is sounded when the white notes are played from A to A. This scale was once called the Aeolian Mode and, with the Ionian Mode (or modern major scale), is a survivor of the ancient modal system (see the Note on Scales and Modes in Book II).

Fig.51

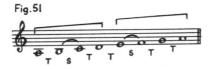

3. The degree-names are the same for the minor as for the major scale.

4. Notice that the order of tones and semitones in the minor scale given in Fig. 51 is T S T – T -- S T T. That is, the two tetrachords are separated by a tone (as in the major scale) but they do not match each other. The order of the intervals in the lower tetrachord is determined by the flattened mediant, the principal feature of the minor scale: this tetrachord is constant. But the upper tetrachord can be varied, allowing considerable flexibility in writing in a minor key (paras. 7 and 9). It may be said that to know the upper tetrachord is to understand the minor scale.

5. The form of the minor scale given in Fig. 51 determines the key-signature. (A minor has neither sharp nor flat.) It may be called the 'modal' form. One of its chief characteristics is that the leading note is a whole tone (not a semitone) below the tonic. At a cadence the result of this is striking. It is less smooth to sing than when the leading note is only a semitone from the final.

Fig.52

Anon.

o - dyr   songe   can   y   not_____   synge

(etc.)

o - dyr songe can y   not _____   synge

Fig.53

6. It became customary for performers, especially singers, to raise the leading note a semitone in certain circumstances in spite of the absence of any accidental to direct this alteration. Such a correction of the written notes was known as *musica ficta*. An interval of one tone was *written* between the seventh degree of the mode and its final: only a semitone was *sung* when, for instance, the voice part fell one step from, and returned to, the final (as in a cadence).

Fig.54

7. The sixth degree of the mode (our submediant) remained unaltered. But the acceptance of the sharpened leading note gave musicians a new form of minor scale which we now call the harmonic minor.

Fig.55

8. The disadvantage of the harmonic minor scale, as well as the characteristic which makes it easy to recognize, is the presence of the augmented second between the sixth and seventh degrees. This interval is awkward to sing in scale passages, though there are no difficulties in playing it on an instrument.

Fig.56

9. Because it is less simple and certainly less natural[1] to sing such an augmented interval, further changes crept in which eventually gave us another form of the minor scale,—the melodic minor. In this scale, when *ascending*, the importance of the raised leading note was recognized and the sixth degree was raised in sympathy to avoid the augmented interval. In *descending*, as there was no reason to disturb either the leading note or the sixth degree, the scale reverted to its original form (the ' modal ' minor).

Fig.57

10. Compare the harmonic and melodic forms of the minor scale. The order of tones and semitones is not very helpful (as in the case of the major scale), and the distinguishing features must be memorized:

   (*i*)   an interval of a minor third from the tonic to the mediant; (harmonic and melodic)

   (*ii*)   an augmented second between the sixth and seventh degrees; (harmonic)

   (*iii*)   the sixth and seventh degrees are sharpened; (melodic *ascending*)

   (*iv*)   the sixth and seventh degrees follow the key-signature; (melodic *descending*)

Exercises

1. Play on the piano harmonic and melodic minor scales in named keys.

2. Write out in named clefs the upper tetrachord of the melodic

---

1 Or, more truly, it evidently *was* less simple and less natural some centuries ago when singing was the principal medium for the performance of music. Today the voice has, to some extent, grown accustomed to imitating the gymnastics of the piano and other instruments.

minor scales of the following keys: (ascending) B, D, F, C:
(descending) E, G, F♯, B♭. Mark the semitone intervals.

3. Write out in named clefs the harmonic minor scales, ascending
and descending, of the following keys: A, E♭, G, F, C. Mark the
semitone and augmented intervals.

4. Sing the following exercises.

Ex.4
(i)

(ii)

(iii)

Hark! how the bells in e-ver-y stee-ple sing, come all— to church good people

Relation to Major Keys

11. The keys of C major and A minor have no sharps or flats. As
the key-signature is the same for both keys, C major is said to be
the relative major of A minor: and A minor the relative minor of
C major.

12. As you will see, the mediant of the minor scale is the tonic of
its relative major. The minor key-signatures should be memorized; but when in doubt remember that the tonic of the minor
key is a minor third below that of its relative major.

13. The cycle of minor keys (in small letters) and their relation
to the major keys (in capital letters) is as follows:

Fig.58

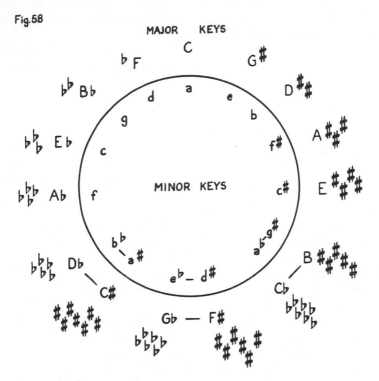

Distinction between Minor Key and Relative Major

14. On looking at a piece of printed music with piano accompaniment there is rarely any doubt as to the key in which it is written. If the signature is two flats, the chords in the piano part in the first and last few bars will usually make it clear whether the music is in G minor or B flat major. But the distinction is less easy when the only source of evidence is the melody. Yet if we wish to add an accompaniment it matters greatly whether the melody is treated as major or minor. The following points will help in making a decision:

(*i*) Look at the final bars and see if the cadence is in the major key to which the signature belongs, or the relative minor: if the leading note is present, does it need an accidental to place it a semitone below the tonic?

(*ii*) Look at the opening bars and see if there is a dominant/ tonic progression in either of the related major or minor keys.

(*iii*) See if the opening bars include a broken tonic chord belonging to either of the possible keys: if so, is the mediant major or minor?

(*iv*) Are there any intervals of an augmented second which could be the sixth and seventh degrees of the harmonic minor scale? Or accidentals which could raise the sixth and seventh degrees of the (ascending) melodic minor scale?

(*v*) Is the possible dominant note of the major key, or the possible leading note of the minor key raised a semitone by an accidental? The former is unlikely: the latter is very possible if the tonic key is minor, for while G♯ is foreign to C major, it is the raised leading note of A minor.

15. It may be misleading to look at the middle of a melody for evidence, especially if it is a long one. Modulations may be made which will remove all traces of the keys we have in mind. Even a search for a half-close may be unhelpful. In a major key it will most likely be in the dominant: but not invariably. In a minor key it may be in the relative major: but there are many exceptions.

Exercises

5. Write down (*i*) the name of the relative minor of the following major keys: D, B, F, E♭, A♭, C♯. (*ii*) the name of the relative major of the following minor keys: E, A, G, B♭, D♭, G♯.

6. Write down the key-signatures of the following minor keys: (in the treble clef) C, E, A♭, B: (in the bass clef) D, E♭, F, A: (in the alto clef) C♯, F♯, G, B♭: (in the tenor clef) D♭, G♭, E, C.

7. Write down the names of the major and minor keys to which given key-signatures belong.

8. Name the key to which the following melodies belong.

Ex.8

9. Transpose the melodies in Exercise 8 into named keys and clefs.

7. CADENCES

1. Cadences, or closes, in music perform the same function as punctuation marks in literature. But it is not possible to say that there is one cadence equivalent to the full-stop, another to the comma, and so on: a musical cadence derives its emphasis, its power to punctuate the flow of the composition, from its context.

2. Though the turn of a melodic phrase may suggest a cadence or close, a cadence from the point of view of the study of harmony is a succession of chords bearing a certain relationship to one another. Two is the minimum requirement. (If there is doubt on this point, ask a player to lift his hands from the keyboard suddenly, in the middle of a phrase: the effect, as in ' musical chairs ', is one of surprise that the music has ended abruptly, without preparation.) In this chapter the cadential relationship will be confined to two chords, but it will soon be realized that the *approach* to the first of these chords is so important that it may more truly be said that a cadence requires three chords to bring

a phrase convincingly to an end.   Notice should therefore be taken of the 'approach' chord: the point will be discussed in greater detail in Chapter 10.

3. The cadences in general use are called perfect, imperfect, and interrupted.

Perfect Cadences

4. A perfect cadence ends on the tonic chord of the key to which the passage permanently or temporarily belongs. Usually this final chord will be in its root position; but sometimes it appears in the first inversion, and the close will on this account be less emphatic, less complete (Chapter 11, para. 12).

5. There are two *principal* forms of the perfect cadence:[1] (*i*) The authentic, in which the progression of the two final chords is from dominant to tonic: V—I.

The dominant chord is in its root position, the bass either falling a fifth or rising a fourth to the tonic. The upper notes can be placed in any order: while the leading note usually rises to the tonic, the movement of the remaining parts will be discussed in Chapter 9. When in a minor key (Fig. 59, (o)) the third of V is usually raised a semitone to form the leading note.

(*ii*) The plagal, in which the progression is from the subdominant to the tonic: IV—I.

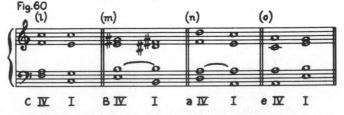

6. In plagal cadences the leading note is missing as it is not contained in the subdominant chord. The movement of the bass, either falling a fourth or rising a fifth, has less vigour than that of

[1] See Note on Cadences in Book II.

the authentic cadence. But this characteristic, combined with the opportunity to repeat or tie over the fifth of IV as the tonic in I (Figs. 60, (l), (m), (n), 61 and 62), give this cadence a colour, a release from tension, and a sense of completion that has an important place in music.

Fig. 61

7. The origin of the plagal form of the perfect cadence, and the context in which it is most often found, is the continuation of a composition (after the sounding of an authentic cadence) on a sustained tonic note or, as it is called, a tonic ' pedal '.

Fig. 62   Lasso

The Imperfect Cadence

8. An imperfect cadence withdraws from the tonic at an inter-mediate point in a composition. It does not establish a new tonality but leaves the ear unsatisfied until the continuation of the work restores the tonic or introduces another key. There are several forms of the imperfect cadence but the most common (and the one which concerns us now) is the progression which moves temporarily to the dominant. This pattern is often referred to as a half-close.

Fig. 63   Pelham Humphrey

D

Fig. 64   Byrd

9. Fig. 63 shows the half-close in its simplest form: an Anglican chant which, while remaining in C major, rests temporarily on the dominant chord at its mid-way point. (There is no modulation: the key is C major throughout.) At Fig. 64, a short Response terminates on a half-close: the Kyrie which follows carries the tonality to its expected conclusion.

10. Longer phrases terminating in an imperfect cadence are taken from Mozart and Haydn.

Fig. 65

Fig. 66

11. The examples quoted should be played until the difference is fully understood between a plagal cadence (in which the tonic is sounded on the final chord) and the half-close (in which the last chord is *never* the tonic).

The Interrupted Cadence

12. A cadence which, on moving towards an authentic ending, interposes one or more chords which delay the full close is called interrupted. Strictly, the progression can only be a cadence if the full close which was interrupted is duly completed; but it is usual to refer to chords up to and including the point of interruption as an interrupted cadence.

Fig. 67

C   I⁵⁴V VI II⁶ I⁶⁴ V   I

13. An interruption can be caused by the sounding of any chord other than the tonic. In practice, the chord of the submediant (VI) is the most common.

Fig. 68

Mozart

B♭   I⁶ II⁶ V VI

Fig. 69

Handel

and | tri – umph o – ver | Death, and thee, | | and | thee, O | Time!

F I V⁷ VI

14. In Parts I and II the interrupted cadences set in exercises will be restricted to the progression V—VI. But note should be taken of other forms in which this cadence appears, and the variety of chords which can cause an interruption. A striking example is given below: in this case the tonic (G major) is dispelled abruptly and is not re-established for another fourteen bars.

Fig.70

Exercises

1. Give the identification in Roman numerals of the four cadences discussed in this chapter.

2. Play on the piano a two-chord version of each of the cadences discussed in this chapter in any named key.

3. Write down the name of the following cadences on hearing them played.

Ex.3

4. Transpose (*i*) at the piano, (*ii*) on paper the examples in Exercise 3 into any named key.

5. Sing the following exercise, noting the cadences.

Ex.5

sa - cred ground __ That shall your forms un-fold, your forms un-fold __ (un-fold) __

8. TIME AND ACCENT

1. Much of the information in this chapter will already be familiar. But it should prove a useful source of reference.

Note-Values

2. It is puzzling to find that the largest unit of time in present-day use is the semibreve, when this is translated as ' half-a-short '. To make clear the origin of the semibreve, the notes of greatest value in common use in the fifteenth century are given in Fig. 71. It was not until the seventeenth century that the smaller units were generally adopted (Fig. 72).

Fig.71

3. While the crotchet and lesser rests may stand anywhere on the stave (within reason), the minim rest lies on the third line and the semibreve rest hangs down from the fourth line; that is, unless the notes of a second voice on the same stave make these positions impossible or confusing to the eye.

4. The dot after a note indicates that its length is to be increased by half its original value:

Fig. 73

5. The double dot after a note indicates that its length is to be increased by half its original value *plus* half of its half:

Fig. 74

Simple Time

6. Time in music is classified as either simple or compound.

7. In simple time, each beat can be divided into two, four or eight subdivisions.

8. If there are two such beats in each bar, the time will be simple duple: if three, simple triple: and if four beats, simple quadruple.

9. Thus, if there are three crotchet beats to a bar, each beat will be divisible into two quavers or four semiquavers, and the time will be simple triple (Fig. 88).

Compound Time

10. In compound time, each beat can be divided into *three*, *six*, or *twelve* subdivisions. That is, each beat will be a *dotted* minim, a *dotted* crotchet, or a *dotted* quaver, indicating that it is readily divisible into three sub-units.

11. If there are two beats (each a dotted unit) in a bar, the time will be compound duple: if three, compound triple: and if four beats, compound quadruple.

12. Thus, if there are two dotted crotchets to a bar, each beat will be divisible into three quavers or six semiquavers, and the time will be compound duple (Fig. 88).

Time-Signatures[1]

13. The denominator (the lower figure) of the time-signature *must* be one of the unit figures given in Fig. 72. That is, it must indicate the unit by which the time will be reckoned in each bar:—

[1] See also Note in Book II.

if the unit be the semibreve, 1: if the unit be the minim, 2: if the crotchet, 4: if the quaver, 8: and if the semiquaver, 16.

14. The denominator MUST be 1, 2, 4, 8 or 16. It CANNOT be 3, 5, 7, or any other such figure.

15. The numerator (the upper figure of the time-signature) indicates the number of units (represented by the denominator) in each bar. In compound time it is necessary to indicate the number of sub-units (paras. 10–12) as it is impossible to describe dotted units. Thus, while in simple duple time the signature may be $\frac{2}{4}$ or $\frac{2}{2}$; in compound duple it must be $\frac{6}{8}$ (that is, $\frac{2}{\rho.}$) or $\frac{6}{4}$ ($\frac{2}{\rho.}$). In simple triple, the signature may be $\frac{3}{8}$, $\frac{3}{4}$ or $\frac{3}{2}$; in compound triple, $\frac{9}{8}$ ($\frac{3}{\rho.}$) or $\frac{9}{4}$ ($\frac{3}{\rho.}$).

16. There is sometimes confusion in choosing a time-signature for a passage in which there are six crotchets in a bar. If each bar is divisible into two, there will be two beats of three crotchets each and the signature must be $\frac{6}{4}$ ($\frac{2}{\rho.}$): but if into three, then there will be three beats of two crotchets each and the signature must be $\frac{3}{2}$ ($\frac{3}{\rho}$).

Fig. 75

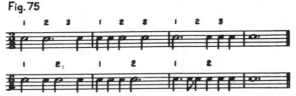

17. If there are six quavers in a bar the same principles apply. Should the bar fall into two the signature must be $\frac{6}{8}$ ($\frac{2}{\rho.}$), and the time is compound duple: but when into three, $\frac{3}{4}$ ($\frac{3}{\rho}$), and the time is simple triple.

18. Whenever the pulse of the music suggests two beats of three sub-units each, then the numerator must be 6: if there are three such beats, 9: if four, 12.

19. By a custom which has an historical foundation, $\frac{4}{4}$ in the time-signature is sometimes replaced by C; and $\frac{2}{2}$ by ₵. The term 'common time', often applied to $\frac{4}{4}$, has nothing to do with the capital C: the appearance of the same letter in both connections is coincidental.

Irregularities

20. It is sometimes necessary to sound three notes, for example, in the space in which, by the time-signature, two or four would normally be written. In such cases, the irregular group uses the

same denomination of note as the regular divisions, and the *number* of notes in the group is written above or below as may be convenient.

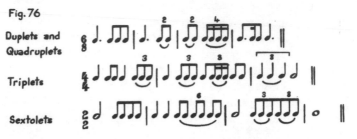

Fig. 76

Duplets and Quadruplets

Triplets

Sextolets

21. Groups of any number of notes may be written in like manner; quintuplets, septolets, and so on.

Fig. 77

Allegro   Vaughan Williams

Fig. 78

Vivace   Wagner

Accent

22. An understanding of the accents which lie within a bar is important in a study of harmony. For example, cadences must have stresses at the most suitable points; suspensions (Chap. 15) must be prepared on a weak beat and sounded on a strong one; and all melodies are dependent on the contrast between strong and weak accents.

23. Strength, as applied to musical accents, is comparative. The term 'strong beat' does not imply a forceful blow: dynamically it may be imperceptible, existing only in the mind of the performer. Too obvious a dynamic accent may ruin a performance. Yet stresses, brought about by a variety of means, are an essential contribution to music.

24. As we listen to the trio from Beethoven's 'Eroica' Symphony (Fig. 50) we feel that four strong beats are sufficient to satisfy the pulse of the phrase (as marked in Fig. 79).

Fig.79

(Vivace)

etc.

25. Yet, as written out by Beethoven, there are apparently twice that number of strong accents because there are twice as many first beats of the bar. This suggests that among first beats in a given series of bars there can be some which (on musical grounds) should receive less accent than others. The scherzo of Beethoven's Ninth Symphony is another example. It moves (for the most part) in four-bar groups: that is, the phrase-stresses are felt every fourth bar.

Fig.80

Beethoven

Molto vivace

etc.

26. Accents within a bar are also flexible. In $\frac{4}{4}$, the first and third beats are generally strong in relation to the second and fourth. Yet often the third beat has to be regarded as weak in comparison with the first; and vice versa. Consider the melodies in Figs. 81 and 82. The speed of the crotchet is approximately the same in both: yet in Fig. 81 the character of the tune calls for stresses on both the first and third beats of each bar; while much of the grace of the phrase in Fig. 82 comes from lifting any trace of stress from the third beat of each bar.

Fig.81

Allegro

Fig.82

Not slow

27. At slower *tempi*, all four beats in common time may gain

prominence; and the quavers may become the sub-units which give relief from the chief stresses.

Fig. 83

Adagio un poco mosso

Beethoven

strings arco

basses pizz.

28. Though in average *tempi* the strong accents of $\frac{4}{4}$ can either be on both the odd beats or on the first alone, in $\frac{2}{4}$ and $\frac{2}{2}$ the first beat will usually be the sole strong accent.

29. In $\frac{3}{4}$ and $\frac{3}{2}$, though the second beat is subsidiary to the first, it is frequently a strong beat in relation to the third.

Fig. 84

Allegro

Purcell

30. In compound time the frequency of accents among the units of each bar will be on the same lines as in simple time. At *allegro*, or even *andante*, $\frac{6}{8}$ and $\frac{6}{4}$ will usually have one strong accent and one weaker accent: $\frac{9}{8}$ and $\frac{9}{4}$ one strong and two weaker accents (with the additional possibility of the second beat being strong in relation to the third).

Fig. 85

Allegro vivace

Mendelssohn

Fig. 86

Andante

Beethoven

31. But again at slower *tempi*, each unit in compound time may well increase its importance with the result that the sub-units (quavers in 6/8 and 9/8; crotchets in 6/4 and 9/4) will be the weak beats. It is impossible to give any firm ruling on this, but whereas 6/8 at *allegro* may carry no more than two harmonies in a bar, a similar passage at *adagio* may be able to carry four harmonies without the effect becoming fussy.

Fig. 87

32. Fig. 88 gives some sample bars (at *tempi* ranging from *andante con moto* to *allegro*) and suggests the most likely units (for counting) and beats (in each bar).

Fig. 88

Sample Bars	Unit	Beats	Signature	Time
	♩	2	2/4	Simple Duple
	♪	3	3/8	Simple Triple
	𝅝	4	4/2	Simple Quadruple
	♩.	2	6/8	Compound Duple
	♩	4	4/4	Simple Quadruple
	𝅗𝅥	3	3/2	" Triple
	♩.	2	6/4	Compound Duple
	♩.	3	9/8	" Triple
	♩	3	3/4	Simple Triple
	♩.	4	12/8	Compound Quadruple
	𝅗𝅥	2	2/2	Simple Duple

Exercises

1. Add bar lines, time-signatures, and phrase-marks to the following.

2. On hearing selected passages played, name the kind of time in which each is written.

3. Having been told the unit in which each passage in Question 2 is written, name the time-signature.

4. Complete the following bars with notes which will produce a satisfactory rhythmic pattern. Add phrase-marks.

Ex. 4

PART II

INTRODUCTORY HARMONY

Harmony is concerned with the study of musical intervals, both singly and in relation to one another.

But intervals are bounded by notes forming chords; so a study of intervals calls for a study of these chords, and the movement of the notes of one chord to those of the next. The relationship between chords is governed by tonality or, as we say, key.

Closely associated with harmony are melody and rhythm. Melody—the predominantly horizontal arrangement of notes— relies constantly on harmony for support and for indications of tonality. Rhythm gives life and meaning to melody and harmony. So while we are considering harmony, close attention must be paid to both melody and rhythm.

9. THE PRINCIPLES OF PART-WRITING

1. A good style in vocal writing is the foundation of musical composition. Once we can think musically in terms of voices we can go on to apply our technique to writing for keyboard, stringed and other instruments. So, unless otherwise directed, all exercises in the remaining chapters of this course should be written for four voices: soprano, alto, tenor, and bass.

2. A part which is well written for the voice can be sung without real difficulty: it is also pleasing to the ear. If you are doubtful about a passage you have written, try singing it: if you cannot, perhaps it is unvocal. Remember that passages well written for the piano or violin do not always make good voice parts, as the following examples prove:

3. The voice can certainly leap with ease. Yet since each interval must be heard in the mind before it is sung, too many leaps in succession (unless they form part of recognizable chords) may make a passage difficult. The leaps in Fig. 91 are not hard to sing as we recognize bars 1 and 2 as a broken chord of C minor, bar 5 as being based on E flat major, and bar 6 on B flat major. In contrast, Fig. 92 may prove awkward to all but the most experienced vocal sight-readers.

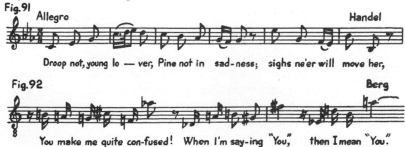

4. The recommendations on part-writing in this chapter are based on the practice followed by composers through more than four centuries. They are not rules laid down without reason and accepted blindly: they are, as it were, a musical code which has been found to satisfy the technical needs and the aesthetic judgment of many of the greatest artists of all time. If a custom was occasionally ignored it was for a special reason. Until you have gained some experience of writing music it will be as well to obey these recommendations strictly. But remember that the final test of the beauty of a passage lies not in a text-book but in the ear of the composer.

Movement of Parts

5. Voice parts should, in general, move by step (that is, by intervals of a second) or by perfect, major, or minor consonant intervals.

6. Movement by step is said to be conjunct: that by intervals of a third or greater than a third, disjunct. When two parts move in opposite directions the motion is said to be contrary: when in the same direction, similar: and when one part remains stationary while another moves, the motion is called oblique.

Fig. 93

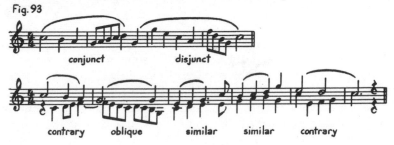

7. The bass moves best in a manner somewhat different from that of the other voices. While too much disjunct motion in the upper parts may produce a restless effect, disjunct motion in the bass is often to be encouraged, especially if it moves contrary to the soprano. This gives strength to the part-writing. Look at the well-known hymn-tune ' St. Anne ': note the intervals sung by the bass, and the contrary motion in the second and third lines. ' York ' tune also shows the grandeur which comes from placing a fine melody on a wide-stepping bass. In this instance root positions only are used: inversions can often ensure a smoother bass line (if that is what is required), but leaps are admissible in the bass more often than in any other voice.

Fig.94

'York'

8. The soprano part usually enjoys a greater freedom than the other voices in an ensemble. The inner parts are, naturally, more restricted in both compass and movement. The following paragraphs on the movement of parts apply to part-writing in general and should be studied closely.

9. A leap to an *accented* note should not normally be made in the same direction as the conjunct motion which precedes it (Fig. 95, (l), (m)). An exception is when the notes which follow the leap return within the interval ((n), (o)). A leap to an *unaccented* note in the same direction as the preceding conjunct motion is usually satisfactory, especially if the notes which follow return within the interval (p). A leap, whether to an accented or an unaccented note, in the opposite direction to a group of steps by conjunct motion is satisfactory (Fig. 96, (q) and (r)).

Fig.95

E

10. The return to the inside of an interval may be delayed for one or more beats, as at Fig. 97 (s).

Fig. 97

Con moto moderato   (s)   Brahms

How love-ly is — Thy dwel-ling place, O Lord _____

11. If a phrase begins with a wide leap, it is better for the continuing phrase to return within that leap.

Fig. 98

f (Baritone Solo)   Walton

Yea, if I pre—fer not Je — ru – sa-lem

Fig. 99

Allegro moderato   Haydn

(strings)

12. If a part must leap a diminished interval, the following note should return within that interval and, if possible, conform to the natural resolution of the chord of which the diminished interval is a part. In Chapter 5, para. 8, reference was made to the resolution of the triad on the leading note: this can be rewritten melodically (Fig. 100 (l)). Compare also (m) and (n) with the quotations in Figs. 101 and 102.

Fig. 100
(l)   (m)   (n)

Fig. 101
Larghetto
(m)   (m)   Handel

the peo-ple that walk-ed, that walk-ed in dark-ness

13. The harmonic resolution of augmented intervals can also be a guide to their melodic use. In these cases the following note continues\in the *same direction* as the leap (though it may well return within it a few beats later).

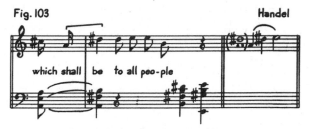

14. To complete this brief reference to the movement of voices and, in particular, to how a phrase continues after a leap of a wide interval, three extracts are quoted from Bach's Mass in B minor—one of the most exhilarating and 'singable' works ever written. At (*i*) the intervals in the first bar are formed from notes of the tonic chord. At (*iii*) the voices again begin with the notes of the tonic chord (B minor): the leap which follows, a minor sixth, is made comfortable for the voices by the subsequent fall within the interval. For the rest, most of the movement in all three extracts is by step. Sing these passages to understand fully how beautiful and how vocal they are.

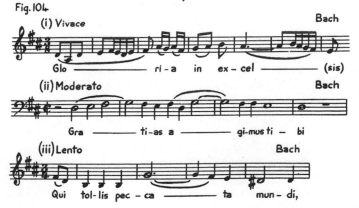

Range

15. Keep within the range which is normal and comfortable for each voice. Even within that range the extreme limits should not often be touched. It must be admitted that composers do some-times call on singers to sing at the limits of their compass for uncomfortably long periods, but there is ample scope within the more usual ranges, and you should not exceed them unless it is absolutely necessary for the musical progression of the parts. In Fig. 105 the semibreves represent the usual limits of each voice: the crotchets are additions for special circumstances. The general movement of the voices may well fall short of all these boundaries by a third or a fourth in each direction.

Fig. 105

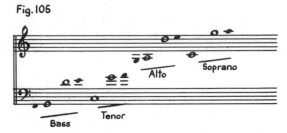

16. The range of each voice overlaps that of the others. In this respect, care must be taken not to invite the basses to sing too near the top of their compass (on which notes they are very strong) while the sopranos are given notes at the bottom of their compass (where they are at their weakest).

Spacing

17. Whenever possible, the four voice parts should be evenly spaced: in what is called the ' extended ' position. Sometimes the three upper parts will group themselves together and the tenor be at a distance of an octave or more from the bass: the position is then said to be ' close '. Most music in which the parts move freely will be a mixture of close and extended writing.

18. It is important to avoid thinking in terms of two hands on the piano keyboard.[1] This can lead to long stretches of writing

[1] There is no objection to using the piano to test exercises after they have been written, or for extemporization: both practices are to be encouraged. But the sounds of the piano must be translated into *vocal* sounds, and the spacing of the chords must be *vocal* spacing. A comparison may be made between the versions of an identical passage in Fig. 106: the one is unvocal, while the other is an example of good choral writing.

in close position, with three parts in the right hand and the bass (often in octaves) in the left. However much we use the piano to play over exercises and examples, it remains an 'unvocal' instrument.

19. Many of the quotations in this chapter are from choral works. In instrumental scores you will find other spacings which may seem to contradict what has been written on the subject. But the tone-quality of voices calls for one approach to spacing: other sounds (orchestral, for example) demand different treatment. Try to imagine (in the mind's ear) how they will sound when played. One of the most beautiful phrases in the whole of classical chamber music is to be found at the opening of Mozart's Clarinet Quintet. On the piano the first three bars sound muddy and uninteresting: sung by four voices there would be a lack of cohesion between the parts: but as intended by Mozart for four solo strings the sound is magical.

20. The opening of the trio of Beethoven's 'Eroica' Symphony (Fig. 50) shows how effective the close spacing of chords can be when sounded on the right instruments. Another well-known passage (the first bars of Tchaikovsky's 'Pathetic' Symphony) is almost ugly on the piano, yet in its orchestral colours it is both expressive and striking.

Fig. 108

Adagio
(Violas)
Tschaikowsky

21. Study these intrumental passages and learn from them. But regard them as forbidden fruit so far as your own writing for voices is concerned.

Doubling

22. To write in four parts with three-note chords, one or more notes of the triad must be doubled: that is, one note (or its octave) must be allotted to two or more voices. In Fig. 109, the chord at (l) has the root in three parts, while the fifth is omitted: at (m) the fifth is doubled. Doubling does not change the name or nature of a chord, provided the bass note remains unaltered.

23. You will find recommendations on the doubling of notes later on as each class of chord is discussed.

Fig. 109 (l)   (m)

Overlapping

Fig. 110 (l)   (n) (o)

(m)

24. In Fig. 110 there are four examples of overlapping: that is, one part has leapt in such a way as to over-reach the note held by a neighbouring part. At (l) the alto overlaps the soprano G by moving from D up to A. The tenor overlaps the bass at (m),

and other examples are at (n) and (o). Such progressions are awkward and produce poor part-writing. They should be avoided.

25. Yet there are (infrequent) occasions when overlapping sounds satisfactory: as, for instance,

(*i*)   when moving between two positions of the same chord:

(*ii*)   in authentic cadences when the dominant in the bass leaps to the same tonic note to which an upper part is moving from the leading note:

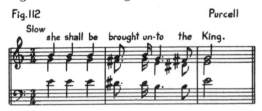

(*iii*)   when overlapping preserves the imitative shape of a phrase:

Crossing of Parts

26. Parts should not cross one another without good reason— for instance to preserve some melodic shape, or to maintain the flow of the part-writing. Thus, the alto and tenor may cross if this improves the movement of the parts: but it must not be imagined that they are two interchangeable, intertwined voices. The bass will rarely rise so high as to cross the tenor or alto parts: and the soprano will not normally sink below the alto line.

27. But there are numerous examples in the works of the great masters in which crossing parts not only sound well but create an effect of extraordinary beauty. In Fig. 114 the passages at (l) and (m) could have been written with no crossing of the soprano by the alto: but anyone who has sung this carol will realize how much of its charm springs from the emergence of the alto from the sustained soprano notes. These are strokes of genius which lift the humdrum on to a higher plane.

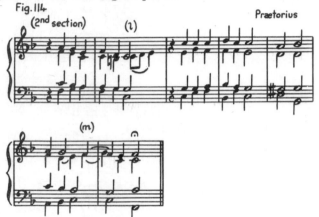

Fig. 114

Praetorius

28. Handel crosses the alto and tenor twice in the quotation at Fig. 115. At (n) he seeks a strong harmony note from which the alto can leap upwards in imitation (not exact) of the other voices: and at (o) the canon between the two middle parts would be interrupted if the voices did *not* cross.

Fig. 115

Handel

29. Finally, in an inspired passage from the ' Credo ' of the Mass in B minor, Bach directs first the chorus basses and then the tenors to march steadily upwards till they overwhelm the other voices in a phrase which speaks confidently of ' the resurrection of the dead '. Only by special means can such awe-inspiring moments be created. Note also that the octave leap by the altos at (s) permits the two sopranos to continue their way to the cadence undisturbed.

Fig. 116

(inst. bass 8va)   re-sur-rec-ti - o - nem mor-tu - o - - - - rum, _____

30. It is in passages such as these that the great composers build up the effect they are seeking. No student is forbidden to do likewise, but the means—especially the unorthodox means—must be justified by the artistry and musicianship of the end.

Forbidden Consecutives[1]

31. There are few ' rules ' in music; but the prohibitions regarding the movement of parts by certain consecutive intervals should be regarded as having the force of law. These are rules which have fewer exceptions than most. Beginners should accept the restrictions and develop a technique which does not violate them. We can all break laws if and when we choose: training and a code of behaviour restrain us. So it is in music.

Consecutive Unisons Fig. 117

poor

[1] See also Note in Book II.

32. No two parts should move in unison with one another in consecutive chords.

33. This does not prevent the sopranos and altos, for instance, singing together for an extended passage. In such a case the part-writing is temporarily reduced from, say, four to three parts.

Consecutive Octaves

34. No two parts should move in octaves with one another in consecutive chords. As with consecutive unisons, this does not apply to extended passages in which octaves between two or more sets of voices are an intentional feature of the composition. Nor does it place any restriction on octave passages on the piano.

35. Exception: Consecutive octaves between two parts are permitted if, in moving by *contrary* motion between the primary chords of the key, one part leaps a fifth and the other a fourth.

Fig. 118

36. A progression between primary chords in which two parts leap from an octave to a unison is usually tolerated (Fig. 119): but it is not good part-writing. The best advice is to avoid all consecutive octaves, octaves to unisons, and unisons to octaves for the time being.

Fig. 119

Consecutive Fifths

37. No two parts should move in fifths with one another in consecutive chords. This applies equally to fifths by *similar* and by *contrary* motion.

Fig. 120

38. Exceptions: (*i*) If the *second* of the two fifths is diminished the progression is good, no matter which parts are involved.

(*ii*) If the *first* of the two fifths is diminished, the progression is good between *upper* parts provided the movement is by step: but is bad between the bass and an upper part.

Fig. 121

Fig. 122

Consecutive Fourths

39. Between upper parts, consecutive fourths are not objectionable (Fig. 28). Between the bass and an upper part they are bad, being dissonances (Chapter 4, paras. 19–23).

40. Exception: Consecutive fourths sometimes occur (and sound well) between the bass and an upper part either when the second chord is itself dissonant, or when the bass includes a passing note.

Fig. 123 (*l*)   (*m*)

41. Consecutive seconds, sevenths, and other consecutive discords should be avoided altogether (but see Chapter 22, para. 4).

Consecutives by Decoration

42. A piece of good part-writing can sometimes be spoiled by the introduction of consecutives when decoration is added to one or more parts. We are free from that danger for the present but the possibility must be mentioned. (Chapter 13, paras. 6 and 12).

Hidden Consecutives

43. The movement of two parts by similar motion to an octave or perfect fifth creates *hidden* consecutives: it is as if the intervening notes had been filled in, revealing the offending interval.

Fig. 124

44. Though hidden consecutive octaves and fifths are inoffensive between upper parts, they should be avoided between extreme parts unless they fall within the exceptions given in paras. 45 and 46.

45. Hidden octaves are permitted
   (*i*) between primary chords in root position, provided the upper part moves by step and the bass rises a fourth or falls a fifth.
   (*ii*) in moving from one position to another of the same chord.
   (*iii*) when the bass moves by step on to the second inversion *of* either the subdominant (IV_4^6) or tonic (I_4^6) chords of the key: that is, when the bass is either the tonic or the dominant with a second inversion superimposed.

Fig. 125

Bb I_4^6 V   G IV_4^6 I

46. Hidden fifths are permitted
   (*iv*) in moving from IV to I provided the upper part moves by step. Unlike the case with hidden octaves, the first chord need not be in root position.

(v) in moving from one position to another of the same chord.

(vi) in moving between the root position of the triads on the supertonic and the dominant, when the third of II falls to the fifth of V.

Fig. 126

6 II V

The Leading Note

47. Melodically the leading note leans towards the tonic at a cadence: and in part-writing it will most commonly obey this natural feeling. But a characteristic of many cadences in chorales harmonized by Bach is that the leading note, when in an inner part, falls to the fifth of the tonic (Figs. 174 and 190). For the present you should allow the leading note to rise in the more usual manner, but when harmonizing chorales in the style of Bach you are at liberty to imitate this feature (Book II, Chapter 35).

10. TRIADS IN ROOT POSITION
(Major Keys)

1. We saw in Chapter 5 that of the triads which can be built on notes of the major scale, three have major thirds (I, IV and V): they are called the primary triads of the key. Three have minor thirds (II, III and VI), and are said to be the secondary triads.

2. The triad on the leading note, VII, was found to be dissonant because of the diminished fifth. It will be discussed in a later chapter.

Primary Triads

Fig.127

I IV V

3. The roots of the primary triads are the tonic (I); the sub-dominant (IV), which can be thought of either as a fifth below the tonic or as one degree below the dominant; and the dominant

(V). If only these three chords are used the bass of a progression must move in some pattern of tonic, subdominant and dominant. For example: Fig 128

I   V   I IV   I IV VI

4. There will be greater freedom in the soprano part, for all notes of the major scale are contained in these three chords.

Movement over a Stationary Bass

5. It is permissible for one chord (on a sustained bass) to support two or more notes of that chord in an upper voice. The result is often more musical than maintaining an unbroken succession of changing chords for every note in the melody.

Fig. 129

6. Here there are *four* notes to each of the first three bars of the melody but only *two* different harmonies in each bar. Look carefully to see which voices remain stationary, and which move. In this chapter and the next, the sign · · · · · will appear whenever one or more of the upper voices can move over a stationary bass: but you should learn to recognize groups of notes which are common to, and are best harmonized by, one chord.

Repeated Notes

7. The rhythm of a passage may sometimes demand the repetition of a chord or an individual note. With the three chords now at our disposal we can harmonize the opening phrase of 'La Marseillaise' as follows:

Fig. 130

8. At (1) we have identical chords to harmonize repeated notes in the soprano: at other points there is movement in the upper parts over a stationary bass. Notice also that the three opening notes on the dominant are not harmonized. It is not possible to lay down any rules about this. These notes could have been harmonized in the usual manner: but bear in mind that it is possible (and, sometimes, musically desirable) to leave such notes unharmonized.

Doubling

9. When doubling a note of a triad in root position to provide four-part harmony, double a primary note of the key rather than a secondary note. And double the root wherever possible in preference to the fifth or third.

10. Thus, in the triads of both I and IV there are two primary notes, the root and the fifth: these should be doubled rather than the third. In V, the root should be doubled if possible (as it is the only primary note in the triad): the fifth may be doubled if the part-writing will be improved by so doing; but avoid doubling the third *which is the leading note of the key.*

11. If it is necessary to omit a note in three- or four-part writing, leave out the fifth. The third is rarely omitted, except at cadence-points in certain styles of the 15th and 16th centuries.

12. As we learn how to use other chords, the recommendations on doubling can be widened. But for the time being, keep to the directions in para. 9 in working your exercises. You should also examine the printed examples in this chapter and see which notes are doubled: play these passages on the piano and try to understand the colour of the individual chords in the context in which they appear. A chord cannot be judged properly in isolation: it should be heard as part of a phrase.

Cadences

13. Here are some arrangements for four voices of the cadences referred to in Chapter 7.

First, the authentic cadence: V—I.

Fig. 131

14. The strength of the authentic cadence derives largely from

the firm march of the bass from dominant to tonic, combined with the rise of the leading note to the tonic. Compare the sound of the cadences in Fig. 131 with that of the following plagal cadences: IV—I.

Fig. 132

C

15. The plagal cadence also has a feeling of completion, but its quality is quite different from that of the authentic. This is due partly to the absence of the leading note in the subdominant chord; partly to the presence of the tonic in both chords (which helps to bind the one to the other); and partly to the fact that the progression of the bass, from subdominant to tonic, is less emphatic.

16. The third cadence which can be built on the primary chords of the scale is the imperfect: I—V. It must be imagined that the tonic has been established and the intention is to withdraw temporarily on to the dominant chord before returning to the tonic: the cadence is incomplete and the pause on the dominant does nothing to disturb the tonality. Play Figs. 63–66 to learn how the half-close is applied in classical music. Using only primary chords it can be harmonized as follows:

Fig. 133

C I V   F I V   G I   V

17. With only the three chords at present at our disposal we can harmonize simple passages which can be musical and interesting. In Fig. 134, notice

(*i*)   the treatment of repeated notes in the melody;

(*ii*)   the binding of some common notes in the alto;

(*iii*)   the placing of the cadences—especially the half-close in the second bar.

Fig. 134

18. In working your own exercises,
    (*i*) be sure to add phrase-marks so that the musical sentences
        are clear to *you* (as the composer).
    (*ii*) make certain of the best points for the cadences; then
        choose the right kind of cadence.
    (*iii*) remember that in an exercise beginning on a weak beat,
        that beat will often carry dominant harmony, especially if
        the strong beat which follows demands a tonic chord.
        Tonality is most firmly established by a dominant/tonic
        progression.
    (*iv*) do not settle finally the spacing of a chord until you have
        made sure of its effect on (at least) the next chord. As in
        chess and draughts, one move in part-writing affects the
        situation several moves ahead. A wrong move and you
        may be heading for disaster. It is sometimes wise to sketch
        in the second chord before the first, the fifth before the
        third and fourth, and so on.
    (*v*) finish by checking your part-writing carefully.

Exercises

1. Add parts for alto and tenor to the following.

Ex. I

2. Add parts for alto, tenor and bass to the following soprano parts.

3. Add three parts above the following basses.

4. Write down the notes sounded by each voice on hearing these chords played on the piano.

5. Sing the following exercise. Name the cadences.

Ex.5

Secondary Triads

Fig. 135

II   III   VI

19. The three secondary triads contain a minor third from the bass. Their addition widens our range of harmonic colour. With six chords our progressions can be smooth and flexible, while remaining as strong as they were before.

Root Progressions with Primary and Secondary Triads

Fig. 136

I   IV I   V   VI   IV V   V   I

20. Much of the strength of the harmonies built only on primary triads came from the wide steps taken by the roots of the chords. In Fig. 136 the least satisfactory moment is in moving from IV to V, the roots being only a tone apart: the remaining intervals are all a fourth or a fifth. The same consideration holds good when secondary as well as primary triads are used. For this reason, the bass in Fig. 137 is good because most of its progression is by steps of a fourth and a fifth.

Fig. 137

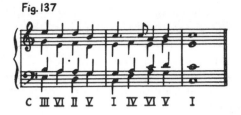

C III VI II V   I IV VI V   I

21. Chord progressions whose roots *fall* by a third sound satisfactory (Fig. 138). In the quotation from Wagner's opera *Parsifal* (Fig. 139) the roots move through I, VI, IV, II, and finally to the tonic.

Fig. 138

I   VI IV II V   III II IV V   I

Fig. 139

p   *cresc.*   *f*   Wagner

22. But if the roots *rise* by a third, it is better if the second of the two can receive the stronger stress. Play Fig. 140 several times, varying the positions of the accents. If the progressions II to IV and III to V are sounded separately you will realize that both are weak. This is not solely because two notes are common to each pair of chords (the same applies to I—III and IV—VI and they sound perfectly satisfactory), but rather because the interval between the roots is a minor third.

Fig. 140

I III V   II IV VI   I IV V   I

23. Greater care is necessary when roots rise or fall by the interval of a second. The closer the roots together, the more thought is needed to ensure a satisfactory progression. (You will see in Chapter 11 that a mixture of root positions and inversions is better than an unbroken line of root progressions: but attention should be paid to the contents of the present paragraphs.)

24. Triads in root position *falling by step* are generally satisfactory, except that

(*i*)   in moving from V to IV, the third of V should not be in the top part: (the effect is better if V is unaccented, but it is not good).

(*ii*)   IV to III (an interval of a semitone between the roots) so rarely sounds well that this progression should be avoided altogether.

Fig. 141
(i)   (ii)

weak;   better but not good: avoid this:

25. Triads *rising by step* are also satisfactory—with the following warnings:

(*i*)   III—IV: the fifth of III (the leading note) should be approached and quitted by step in *contrary* motion to the rising root.

(*ii*)   IV—V: the thirds of these chords should not both be in the top part. That is, if the given bass (in C major) is F—G, do not write A—B in the soprano: if A—B are given in the treble, do not use IV—V under them, but write II—V, or VI—V.

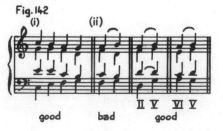

Fig. 142
(i)   (ii)

                              II V   VI V
good   bad   good

Interrupted Cadence

26. This, as shown in Chapter 7, is the arresting of an (apparent) authentic cadence by some chord other than I after V—though exercises in its use will, in this volume, be restricted to progressions moving to VI. (Fig. 143 below and Figs. 67–69).

27. In Fig. 144 the sequence V—VI occurs twice. Play this passage and note the difference between the two. The ear will analyse V—VI in bar 1 as part of a free-running phrase unconnected with any cadence: but the same progression in bar 2 is instantly recognizable as an interruption to an authentic cadence. This is largely because of the placing of V on the final beat of one bar and the sounding of VI on the succeeding strong beat.

28. Note also that, in Figs. 143 and 144, the third of VI (a primary note) is doubled—with an entirely satisfactory effect.

29. In the course of experiments at the keyboard (a most necessary exercise) you will find other chords which, following V, interrupt the normal march of an authentic cadence. Do not be satisfied

with any progression which completely disrupts the music or offends against an accepted artistic standard. Chord sequences which sound harsh, weak, or uneasy should be noted—and avoided in subsequent written work. Personal experience in matters affecting the judgement of the ear is worth dozens of printed paragraphs.

Doubling

30. The recommendations in para. 9 apply equally to secondary triads. Double a primary note or the root whenever possible. In III, the third (being a primary note) can be doubled with good effect; whereas to double the fifth (the leading note of the key) will almost certainly create difficulties as regards consecutives.

Approach Chords

32. The secondary triads provide additional approach chords to the four cadence patterns: authentic, plagal, imperfect and interrupted. We know already that roots proceeding in wide steps give a good effect, so II—V—I; II—IV—I; or II—IV—I—V will sound well. And VI is a good approach to any of these cadences. IV—V—I (para. 25); and V—IV—I (para. 24) are also good. There remains III. The triad on the mediant is unconvincing and weak before V—I (where the root is rising by a minor third): but it is a satisfactory approach to I—V; and IV—I (para. 25 (i)).

Fig. 145

The Triad on the Mediant

33. The difficulties in approaching or quitting III in root position are no good reason for not using this chord. It has many virtues. Learn the progressions which should be avoided and then let III take its natural place among the chords at your disposal.

Exercises

6. Write down a list of the root progressions in which III is (*i*) satisfactory; (*ii*) to be avoided.

7. Write down the root progressions which call for special care; and add the recommendations (as given in paras. 20–25).

8. Complete the following by adding parts for alto and tenor.

9. Add parts for alto, tenor, and bass below the following soprano parts.

10. Add parts for soprano, alto, and tenor above the following basses.

Ex. 10

11. Write passages in named keys on the following root progressions. Pay attention to the time, melody and rhythm. Include one cadence at an intermediate point. Add phrase-marks.

   (*i*) V¹ I I V VI¹ IV I I¹ IV II V III¹ VI V¹ I

   (*ii*) ¹I VI II¹ V I¹ I IV II¹ V I¹ IV V¹ I

   (*iii*) V¹ I IV¹ I VI II¹ V VI¹ II V V¹ I VI II V¹ I

   (*iv*) ¹I V III VI¹ IV I V¹ I VI II V¹ V I

   (*v*) I I III VI IV II V VI III VI I VI II IV I

   (*vi*) V V I I V VI I IV II V I V V I I IV II V VI IV V I

12. Write down given passages from dictation. (Passages for dictation, covering the work of Chapters 10–21, are to be found at the end of Book II.)

II. TRIADS IN THE FIRST INVERSION
(Major Keys)

1. The first inversions of all triads in a major key are consonant. So we can add seven new chords to the six triads in root position with which we worked exercises in Chapter 10.

2. A first inversion (or chord of the sixth) has a different sound from the root position of the same triad. But both chords have the *same root*. In the $\frac{5}{3}$ chord the root and bass are the same note: in I⁶, II⁶, III⁶ and the rest, the root is in an upper part and the bass note is the third of the root.

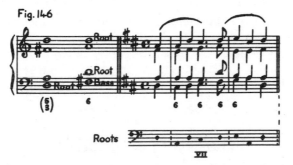

Fig. 146

3. With these seven chords, good part-writing will depend on mixing first inversions with triads in root position. The recommendations in Chapter 10 still hold good: wide intervals between roots sound well, though smaller intervals may be satisfactory. But the substitution of a first inversion for a $\frac{5}{3}$ can often make the bass line more smooth. Thus, in Fig. 146 the bass moves by step until the final cadence: yet some of the roots of this passage are separated by wide intervals. (Note the inclusion of VII⁶.)

Fig. 147

4. Compare the bass line of Fig. 146 with the harmonization of

the same melody (Fig. 147) which uses only root positions. Both are good: but it is not difficult to realize that the chord of the sixth opens up new possibilities in harmonic colour. The wide steps of the bass of Fig. 147 may be suitable on occasions (as in 'York' tune, Fig. 94), yet the smoother progression in the first example is better for normal use.

Doubling

5. Primary notes of the $\frac{6}{3}$ chord should be doubled in preference to other notes. This agrees with the recommendation regarding root positions in Chapter 10, para. 9. Further, the sixth can be doubled; except that of VII⁶, which is the leading note of the key. The third of the chord can also be doubled with good effect. As this is the fifth of the root, there is an important difference in this respect between the $\frac{6}{3}$ and $\frac{5}{3}$.

6. It is not always satisfactory to double in an inner part the bass note of a first inversion (the third of the root). On the other hand, if the *melody* doubles the bass and moves by contrary motion, the effect is usually good. Other instances will also arise in which the smooth line of the part-writing justifies the doubling of the bass.

Fig. 148   Hanover

Fig. 149   'Psalm 68'

Omitting a Note

7. If one note of a first inversion has to be omitted in three- or four-part writing, avoid omitting the third (the fifth of the root). To do so produces a thin, unsatisfactory sound. In root position the fifth may well be left out (Chapter 10, para. 11) but not in the case of chords of the sixth.

The $\frac{6}{3}$ in Sequence

8. Chords of the sixth in sequence are permissible and effective, especially in three-part writing. (It is hardly necessary to draw attention to the dangers of writing consecutive $\frac{6}{3}$ s if the third is sounded *above* the sixth.)

Fig. 150   Palestrina

Fi - li- um De- i   u - ni - ge- ni- tum

9. In four parts some care is needed to avoid forbidden consecutives being produced by the free (the fourth) voice. In Fig. 151 (*i*), the alto's progression by sixths and fourths is awkward: and the parallel thirds between the bass and tenor move too low (in bar 2) and will create a thick, unpleasing sound. At (*ii*), the alto is not much improved: but the thick effect in the bass is dispelled by freeing the tenor.

10. The progression at (*iii*) is best: the three parts carrying the parallel notes of the $\frac{6}{3}$ s are well spaced: and the tenor part, while disjunct, is built on simple intervals. (When only two chords of the sixth are sounded in sequence, the fourth voice should, if possible, move by contrary motion).

Fig. 151
(i)   (ii)   (iii)

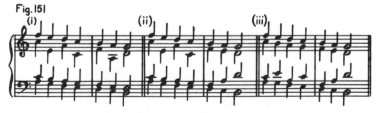

Approach Chords

11. Chords of the sixth can be used as approach chords to cadences. They are most frequently included when the bass is in a position to move by step to V, to IV or to I (according to the cadence to be sounded). Thus, II⁶ and IV⁶ are good approaches to V. I⁶—IV is satisfactory. But III⁶—IV calls for care. (There is no reason to avoid this progression altogether: but let the leading note rise or, if it must be doubled, let one rise and the other fall to the third of IV. If the bass is doubled, follow the advice given in para. 6.) V⁶ and VII⁶ can precede the imperfect cadence.

Fig. 152

Inverted Cadences

12. The part-writing or the musical context will sometimes call for a chord of the sixth in place of a root triad as the final or penultimate chord of a cadence. This does not create a new cadence but only an irregular version of one we already know. If the examples in Fig. 153 are played, they will be found to be less emphatic than the regular patterns. These inverted cadences should be used sparingly: but they have a place in music and deserve mention.

Fig. 153   Fig. 154   Handel

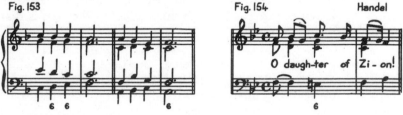

Establishment of a Key

13. Good part-writing, it was said in para. 3, calls for the mixing of root positions and first inversions. A good bass line will include movement by step and by leap. We must now consider what chords should be chosen, why they should be chosen, and when.

14. If we play a chord, any chord, by itself we do not know to what tonic it is related. The triad of D major can be the tonic of that key: but it can also be AIV, GV, bIII, f♯VI, or eVII. Other chords must be sounded before we can tell the relationship of our original triad to this or that key.

15. We know that the dominant and subdominant are the strongest supporters of a tonic chord. The secondary triads give colour and contrast to the harmonization of a phrase, but without V and IV they cannot tell us what key we are in.

16. When harmonizing a passage establish the key in the course of the first phrase. Leave no doubt as to the key-centre of the composition. After this has been done there is much to be said for

introducing chords less closely connected with the tonic (the secondary triads) before re-affirming the tonality for the final cadence. In Fig. 147 the first four chords read V I I V: they have established the tonic before a pause is made on a half-close. We are now certain of the central key. After that, two secondary chords take us a little further from (but still within hearing of) the 'home' key, and give contrast by introducing for the first time the colour of the minor triad. Finally, the dominant chord re-asserts the tonic, and the passage ends in an authentic cadence. The same process takes place in Fig. 146. Here the tonic is established in the first three chords: there is no half-close but a halt on VII^6, which leads away towards II^6 before the return to the final tonic cadence.

17. Compare these two root progressions:

$$\text{Fig. 146} \quad \text{I} \mid \text{V I VII} \parallel \text{I} \mid \text{II V I}$$
$$\text{Fig. 147} \quad \text{V} \mid \text{I I V} \parallel \text{VI} \mid \text{II V I}$$

18. This subject is important: it is the basis of musical composition. A choice of chords must not be haphazard. Just as this short phrase has, in two bars, moved from and back to a key-centre, so longer compositions change their relationship to the 'home' key, sometimes moving away some distance, or modulating to a new key. The more chords we have to choose from, the greater must be our care

(*i*)   to establish the key of the composition; then

(*ii*)   to introduce chords whose roots are less closely associated with the tonic; and

(*iii*)   to return to the original key and re-establish it by chords of the dominant (sometimes supported by the subdominant).

Exercises

1. Complete the upper notes of the chords of the sixth in the following exercises.

(iii)

2. Write phrases in four parts to correspond with the following figures.

Ex.2

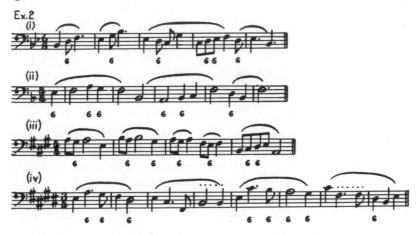

3. Add three parts below.

Ex.3

4. Add three parts above.

Ex.4

5. Sing the following exercise. Listen carefully to the difference in sound between root positions and chords of the sixth.

Ex.5 Andante

'Twas in the flow'ry Spring, The lin-net, nightingale and thrush, Most

sweetly they did sing, sat on the fresh green___ hawthorn bush.

6. Write out Exercise 5 in a named (different) key: describe each chord (with Roman numerals).

7. Write down given passages from dictation.

12. TWO-PART WRITING

1. So far we have been mainly concerned with the vertical aspect of chords. We know that their relationship to one another must be controlled: by avoiding certain consecutives and complying with various customs governing the movement of the parts. But attention to the vertical composition of our exercises has prevented us giving more than a glance at the horizontal texture. Now we are to consider the horizontal movement of two parts: but in doing so, we must not lose sight of the vertical relationship between one note and another.

2. The chords which can be used are those we have discussed in the last two chapters: the triads of the major keys in their root position and first inversion. But while in writing in four parts one note (at least) of a three-note chord must be doubled, in writing for only two parts one note (at least) of the same chord must be omitted. Two notes must imply a three-note chord.

Fig. 155

3. If we harmonize this melody for four voices using the chords we already know, we shall need three different harmonies in the 1st and 3rd bars; at least two in the 2nd; and as many as four harmonies in the 4th and 5th bars. Even at *allegretto* the effect will be rather restless.

Fig. 156

4. If, instead of a full harmonization, we add only *one* part below the same melody we have greater freedom. In Fig. 157 by using

sixths and thirds, with only an occasional octave, we can write a second part which fits the melody well, has character of its own, and is as smooth and singable as the melody itself.

Fig. 157

5. Compare the bass of the four-part version with that of the duet. The latter moves largely by step. It may lack the boldness of the four-part bass, yet it gains immeasurably in sweetness. Moreover, the duet is clearly the laying together of two horizontal parts of similar quality with a minimum of emphasis on the vertical aspect of the writing: on the other hand, the four-part setting is essentially a series of chords, and the three lower voices have not the same character or freedom of movement as the melody.

6. We say that Fig. 156 is an example of harmony, and that the duet is what is known as counterpoint. This is true. But it is sometimes thought that harmony and counterpoint are two separate musical sciences: that music can be written in the one style or in the other; but never in both at once. This is far from the truth. Harmony is certainly built vertically: yet the parts should be so arranged that they flow as contrapuntally as possible, which means that attention must be paid to their horizontal movement. Counterpoint, by contrast, is mainly horizontal in structure and can be thought of as the weaving of several threads of sound: but counterpoint cannot ignore the vertical relationship of one part to another. A study of counterpoint is necessary in order to write pleasing harmony: and an understanding of harmony is equally necessary if the parts are to combine in satisfactory counterpoint.

7. You will recognize the hymn-tune printed below. It is an example of harmonic writing as it is a succession of chords which support a melody: yet it contains a contrapuntal device which is well known, or which can be discovered by looking closely.

Fig. 158   Tallis

(etc.)

8. In writing in two parts it is best to mingle thirds and sixths, and to use fifths and octaves sparingly. The fifth, except at the beginning and end of a piece, should be placed on an unaccented beat and approached by contrary motion. Leaps are neither prohibited nor discouraged; but the inclusion of some step-wise movement will help to produce parts most suitable for singing. Similar motion is good provided it is relieved and strengthened by contrary motion. One part can move while the other remains stationary (oblique) provided (at present) all the intervals are consonant. Sequences sound well, though it is seldom wise to repeat a phrase more than once without introducing some melodic or rhythmic variation.

Fig.159

9. When both voices begin simultaneously it is usual for them to be an octave, a fifth or a third apart. A sixth, though not wrong, is less often found.

Implied Chords

10. Try to hear in your mind's ear the full chord implied by the notes of the two voices. If the root progression would be unsatisfactory in four-part writing it will be equally so in two parts. Look at Fig. 160 then compare it with the next example in which the implied chords have been written in and the root progression added below. Note that the key of B flat is firmly established in the first two bars, after which secondary triads are introduced as a contrast (Chapter 11, paras. 13–18).

Fig.160

Fig. 161

key establishment.

11. In oblique motion all intervals must (at present) be consonant. If a part leaps it must do so either to another note of the implied chord, or to a note which will imply a fresh (and suitable) chord. Examples of the former are (in Fig. 162) at (l), (m) and (n). The moving part suggests a second harmony at (o), (p) and (r): and at (q) three chords are outlined. The progression at (s) is permitted since two consonant chords are implied: the passage resembles a second inversion sounded as a broken chord (and it would be if the E were sustained) but it is a chord of I⁶ moving to VI.

Fig. 162

implied harmony

Cadences

12. When the leading note in the upper part rises to the tonic at a cadence, the bass may move from the dominant to the tonic in the usual way (V—I). A more smooth progression, and one well suited to our early exercises in counterpoint, is for the lower part to move downwards from the supertonic to the tonic. The implied chord is VII⁶ (Fig. 163): the complete cadence is VII⁶—I. (See also Fig. 52.) The inversion of this form of cadence is equally good: here the lower voice will sound the leading note and the upper part will fall by step to the tonic or rise to the mediant. The implied chord is VII (in root position) but *without the diminished fifth* (Figs. 164 and 165). (A Note on this cadence is included in Book II).

Fig. 163   Gibbons

an an-swere I will make;

F VII⁶ I

Fig. 164   Morley

E'en those darts my sweet Phil-lis

Fig. 165   Morley

dal - ly, dal-ly, dal-ly, dal-ly, dal-ly.

Exercises

1. Add a second voice (in a named clef) below.

Ex.1
(i)
add A or B.
(ii)
add A.
(iii)
add B.
(iv)
add A.

2. Add a second voice (in a named clef) above.

Ex.2
(i)
add S.
(ii)
add A.⁵⁸
(iii)
add S.

(iv)

add S.

3. Work the passages in Exercises 1 and 2 at the piano.

Imitation

13. One of the chief characteristics of contrapuntal writing is the possibility of making the individual voices distinct by (*i*) beginning one part before another and (*ii*) introducing into the second part an imitation of the melodic and rhythmic shape of the first part. You may therefore delay the entry of a contrapuntal part a few beats especially if, by so doing, it becomes possible to imitate the voice which is already sounding.

14. In Fig. 158, the melody in the tenor is imitated in the soprano one bar later. As this imitation is exact from beginning to end it is called a ' canon '. Other well-known canons, or ' rounds ', are 'Three Blind Mice ' and ' Sumer is i-cumen in '. But we are not at present concerned with canons. Imitation need not be exact or everlasting: it is sufficient if only the first few notes in one voice are repeated in the voice which follows—either at the same, or at a different, pitch. Thus:

Fig. 166

Allegro vivace   Bach

(piano)

Fig. 167   Morley

Sop. I

Go ye my can-zo-nets to   my dear dar - - - - -   ling, Go ye my

Sop II

Go ye my can-zo - nets to my dear dar - - - - -

can-zo-nets to   my dear dar - - - - - - -   ling.

- - - ling, dear dar - ling,   Go ye my can-zo - nets to

15. The imitation in Fig. 166 is at the interval of an octave, and is continued for two bars: the two parts then go their ways independently. The imitation in Fig. 167 lasts for longer. The entry by the first voice in bar 1 on the tonic is answered by the second voice on the dominant: the dominant entry in bar 4 is again answered by a tonic entry in bar 7.

16. Imitation (or, as is often said, a point of imitation) may be introduced on any degree of the scale. But for the present we will confine ourselves to imitation at the octave, and to cases in which the tonic is answered by dominant, and dominant by tonic. This can quite easily be done within the limits of the chords with which we are now familiar. It will soon be found that imitative writing adds greatly to the interest of the completed exercises.

Fig.168

17. You should examine all two-part exercises and see if there is a workable point of imitation. Exercises (and examination questions) are often constructed in such a manner that the discovery of the entry point for the imitation is the key to the problem. But not always. Do not introduce imitation forcibly if all the signs indicate that it will not fit. And beware of carrying the imitation beyond the point at which it ceases to work satisfactorily.

18. For the remainder of this chapter, and in Chapters 14 and 15, exercises in which a point of imitation will fit are marked ↝. After that you will be expected to study the given part and decide for yourself.

Exercises

4. Add a second part (in a named clef) below. On completion, write in the Roman numerals of the implied chords.

Ex. 4

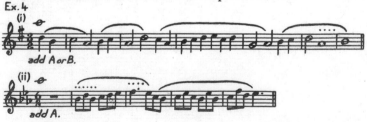

5. Add a second part (in a named clef) above. On completion, describe the implied chords by Roman numerals.

6. Sing the following: then write down the chords implied.

7. Write down given passages from dictation.

13. A. UNACCENTED PASSING NOTES
B. UNACCENTED AUXILIARY NOTES
C. ADDITIONAL HARMONY NOTES

A. *Unaccented Passing Notes*

1. So far, our exercises have been ' note for note ': all the notes of a chord have been sounded together and sustained until the next chord. The only exception has been the freedom to move the upper notes of a chord to other notes of the same chord over a stationary bass.

2. We are now to introduce unessential diatonic notes which join two successive harmony (or essential) notes of the same part by step-wise motion. Called unaccented passing notes, they are sounded on unaccented beats of the bar and *are not harmonized.* For example, the interval of a third between two harmony notes of the same voice can be filled by the diatonic note lying in between ((l) and (m) below).   Other intervals can be filled in a similar manner ((n) and (o)).

Fig. 169

You will see from (m) that not only is the passing note, C, not harmonized, but the dissonant interval between it and the bass is ignored. The consonance of the chords of G and D satisfies the ear.

3. Unaccented passing notes can be in simple or compound time, in any rhythm, and in any voice. They can also be sounded by more than one voice at a time, either by similar or contrary motion. But all passing notes must be approached and quitted by step.

Fig. 170

4. If you play Fig. 170, you will feel at once that the second half sounds more flowing—on account of the inclusion of several passing notes. Experience and musicianship are the only guides on when and when not to link melodic intervals by passing notes. Too many may produce a restless feeling: and badly placed ones may diminish the effectiveness of those in the best context. Passing notes are an additional piece of equipment: the use of this equipment calls for discrimination and artistry.

5. Passing notes in more than one part at a time by parallel motion present little difficulty. By contrary motion they can also be satisfactory, though care is needed. But two sets of passing notes by contrary motion, each correct in itself, may produce discordant effects which must be regarded as outside our scope at present (Fig. 172). While working through this book unaccented passing notes should be written in not more than two parts at a time by similar motion.

Fig. 171

Vaughan Williams

found, Just as the tide was flow — ing.

Fig. 172

Blow

our de — fen — der

6. A danger in writing passing notes is that forbidden consecutives may appear between two parts. A progression composed of an interval of a sixth followed by one of a fifth, for example, is satisfactory in many circumstances; yet the introduction of a passing note may disclose consecutive fifths. Thus:

Fig. 173

7. One can often introduce a passing note in an authentic cadence between the root of V (in an upper voice) and the third of I (Fig. 174). There is no objection to this progression, unless it is used so much as to tire the ear with its frequency. Both Bach and Handel use it: but on numberless occasions they have ignored the opportunity to do so. We shall do well to exercise similar moderation.

Fig. 174   Bach

V^{87} I

Exercises

1. Rewrite the following to include some unaccented passing notes.

Ex.1

(i)

(ii)

(iii)

2. Add three parts below. Begin by marking those notes which can be treated as unaccented passing notes.

Ex.2

3. Add three parts above. Mark the unaccented passing notes: also include some in your melody.

Ex.3

4. Add a second part (in a named clef) below. Include some passing notes.

Ex.4

add A.

add A or B.

5. Add a second part above. Include some passing notes.

add S.

add S.

B. Unaccented Auxiliary Notes

8. Passing notes move by step from and to a harmony note. Unaccented auxiliary notes move upwards or downwards by step from a harmony note and *return to the same note*. They are unessential and are not part of the harmony.

9. Both passing notes and auxiliaries are forms of musical decoration. They are frequently to be found in combination with one another. For instance, by their inclusion, a bare progression of triads in root position is converted by Purcell into a passage of great beauty.

Fig. 176

I V II VI

10. Auxiliaries can appear in more than one part at the same time. They are normally diatonic, rising or falling by intervals of a tone or a semitone. Sometimes the fall of a whole tone is judged (by the ear) to be too wide an interval and the auxiliary is then raised a semitone, chromatically. (Similarly, if the rise of a whole tone is unpleasing, the auxiliary may be lowered a semitone.) There is no fixed rule on this point. The judgement of the ear and the musical style of the period must be the guides. Play Fig. 177 as written: then repeat it, omitting the accidentals so that all notes are diatonic. Compare the two versions, remembering that Mozart preferred the fall of only a semitone.

Fig. 177

11. When raising or lowering one auxiliary chromatically all others in the same chord should be similarly altered, unless the interval is already that of a semitone. Beethoven wrote both C sharp and A sharp in Fig. 178 (*i*): he did not write the passage at (*ii*).

Fig. 178

12. Like passing notes, auxiliaries can produce forbidden consecutives in an otherwise satisfactory passage. Count the forbidden parallels in Fig. 179 (*ii*).

Fig. 179

13. We have said that auxiliary notes are a form of musical ornament. There are a number of ornaments which are built on auxiliary notes alone. The commonest of these is the plain shake, or trill, in which the auxiliary and harmony notes alternate rapidly several times. There are other well known patterns of ornament which will be seen in classical music: here is a table of them, with the names by which they are usually known.

Fig. 180

NAME	SIGN	PLAYED
Plain Shake, or Trill		
Shake with Turn		
Mordent		
Upper Mordent		
Turn (over a note)		
Turn (between two notes)		

❋ These ornaments require the auxiliary to be accented.

Exercises

6. Introduce unaccented auxiliary notes at suitable points. Do not add passing notes.

Ex.6

C. *Additional Harmony Notes*

14. When, in Chapter 10, para. 5, we referred to the possibility of a part moving to another harmony note over a stationary bass, it was an introduction to the use of additional harmony notes. While unaccented passing notes are not harmony notes and are always approached and quitted by step, an additional harmony note can only be approached by a leap from another note of the

same chord, though it can be quitted by step (to another chord).

15. Additional harmony notes can be sounded in the bass, though care will have to be exercised in moving to the next chord (Fig. 181). Leaps of a fourth or fifth may result in ambiguous harmony, or suggest the use of the second inversion of the triad.

16. Additional harmony notes can be effective both melodically and rhythmically. Their name is not important, but you should remember their existence.

Fig. 181

Fig. 182

Exercises

7. Study the following quotations: mark the essential harmony notes, and then the passing, auxiliary, and additional harmony notes.

(The exercises which follow contain unaccented passing notes, unaccented auxiliary notes and additional harmony notes.)
8. Add three parts below.

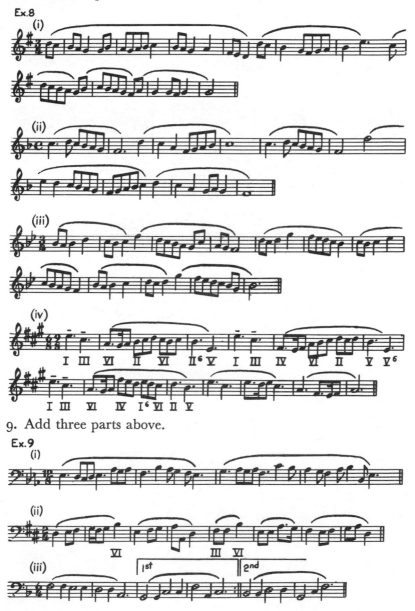

9. Add three parts above.

10. Add a second part below.

11. Add a second part above.

12. Write down given passages from dictation.

14. TRIADS IN MINOR KEYS
(Root Position and First Inversion)

Root Position

1. In building triads in a minor key both the ascending and the descending forms of the *melodic* scale must be taken into account. The sixth and seventh degrees of the scale will, in an ascending melodic phrase, be raised by a semitone: but in a descending phrase they will agree with the key-signature (Fig. 57). So there can be more than seven triads in root position in a minor scale, though some of them are unsuitable for our present purpose.

Fig. 183

2. In Fig. 183, the consonant triads we can use are: I; IV (with either the raised or the flattened sixth degree); V (with either the raised or the flattened leading note); III, VI, and VII built on the descending scale; and II built on the ascending scale. Nine triads in all.

Fig. 184

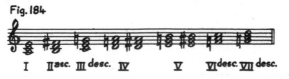

3. Note that V^asc is the only consonant triad with the raised leading note. When a melody in the top line has the raised sixth and seventh degrees, V^asc can be preceded by II^asc (Fig. 185 (i)). IV^asc would be unsuitable here as the submediant and the leading note are the thirds, respectively, of these chords (Chap. 10, para. 25). But if the raised leading note is approached from *above*, it is best to *flatten* the sixth degree in the chords which precede it. These two notes, it will be remembered, sound an augmented interval, which is a strong feature of the harmonic minor scale: they help to stress the minor mood of the passage. Minor (authentic)

cadences almost invariably include the flattened sixth (Fig. 185 (ii)).

(The references to the ascending and descending forms of the minor scale in Figs. 183 and 184 are not part of the system of figured bass. They should be omitted as soon as the existence of this variety of chords is understood. Learn to recognize—and avoid—triads with augmented or diminished fifths. When in doubt, check the figuring of the fifth. The only triad we are now using which requires an accidental to form a perfect fifth, is II^{asc}.)

4. The principles of part-writing are applied to the minor keys in the same manner as to the major. But there are two important points to note.

(*i*) Too much insistence on the *descending* form of the minor scale may give a feeling of being in the relative major; for the flattened seventh is the dominant of the relative major. The minor key must be re-established when necessary by the introduction of either the sharpened leading note in a chord (V), or by a melodic phrase containing the raised sixth and seventh degrees. In Fig. 186, the relative major gradually asserts itself until, in bar 4, it becomes established: and a modulation from B minor to D major has been effected. In Fig. 187, the tonic key of B minor has been preserved by introducing VI^{desc} and IV^{desc} followed by V^{asc}.

Fig. 186

Fig. 187   TRIADS IN MINOR KEYS   109

(*ii*) Avoid the melodic use of augmented intervals. It is better to write a diminished interval and to return by step within the interval on the following beat.

Fig. 188

5. Accidentals are frequently needed in a minor key, even when the writing is diatonic. The figuring may for this reason require ♮, ♯ or ♭ to indicate the alteration of the third of the chord. Sometimes, as in II^{asc}, an accidental must also be applied to the fifth: II$^{♯5}$.

Exercises

1. Write out the triads in root position you are free to use in the following minor keys:

> c, e, g, f♯, f♮, d, and b.

2. Analyse the chords used in Figs. 185 and 187.

3. Harmonize the following cadences, using only triads in root position.

Ex. 3.

6. In certain styles of music, especially those written between 15th and 18th centuries, the final chord of a passage in the minor key is often given a major third. This substitution of a major for a minor triad is called a *tierce de Picardie* or Picardy third. It should not be used indiscriminately: a cadence can be just as effective when ending on a minor chord.

Fig. 189   Byrd

Fig. 190   Bach

First Inversion

Fig. 191

I⁶ II⁶ II⁶♯ III⁶ III⁶♯ IV⁶ IV⁶ V⁶ V⁶ VI⁶ VI♯ VII⁶ VII♯
desc. asc. desc. asc.

7. The first inversion of all triads in a minor key, whether the sixth or seventh degrees be raised or flattened, is consonant (Fig. 191). The only one which, though consonant, should not be used at present is III⁶♯: this, the inversion of the triad containing an augmented fifth, comprises two intervals of four semitones each. No great harm will arise if it *is* used; but it requires special handling (Chapter 17, para. 13).

8. A passage in a minor key should be harmonized by a mixture of first inversions and triads in root position, as in the case of major keys. It is as necessary, when using first inversions, to include some instances of the raised sixth and seventh degrees, as it was with root

positions only (para. 4). The same care should be taken to avoid augmented melodic intervals in the top and bass parts. There is less objection to them in inner parts, though their absence will add to the smoothness of the part-writing. Diminished intervals are preferable to augmented in almost all circumstances (para. 4).

Two-part Writing

Fig. 192

9. In each example in Fig. 192 the G♯ is the lowest note (by a semitone) of a melodic phrase coming from above: and the F♮ is the highest note (also by a semitone) of a phrase in the alto part coming from below. This feature of working in a minor key has already been discussed in para. 3: it is equally important in two-part writing. In the following passage the upper part dips three times by an interval of a semitone below the tonic, and sounds the raised leading note: the lower part moves between the lower tonic and the dominant, and twice exceeds this range by an interval of a semitone only and so sounds the flattened sixth degree. (If in doubt as to whether A♯ and G♮ are 'right', play each part separately substituting A♮ and G♯: and then play both parts together with these altered notes.)

Fig. 193

Exercises

(using first inversions and triads in root position)

4. Complete the following cadences.

Ex. 4

5. Add three parts below.

Ex. 5

6. Add three parts above.

Ex. 6

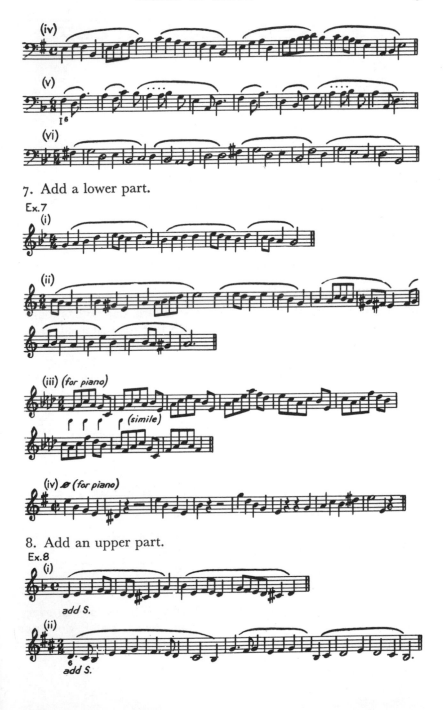

7. Add a lower part.

8. Add an upper part.

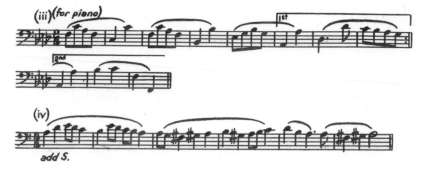

9. Work Exercises 5, 6, 7, and 8 at the piano.
10. Write down given passages from dictation.

15. SUSPENSIONS

1. A note common to two or more chords in the same voice can, often with advantage, be tied over so as to form one note of longer duration (Figs. 62 and 134). So far such tied (or sustained) notes have always been harmony notes. But one or more notes of a chord can also be tied over to a non-harmony note: that is to say, it can remain stationary until after the remaining voices have moved to a chord of which it is not a part.

2. In the following passage the first two beats of every bar of the melody are sustained by a minim, and are part of either a $\frac{5}{3}$ or a $\frac{6}{3}$ chord:

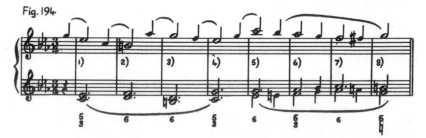

Fig. 194

3. Now it is possible to tie the third beat of the melody in every bar to the first beat of the succeeding bar so that it does not sound the new harmony until the second beat. These tied notes are 'suspended'.

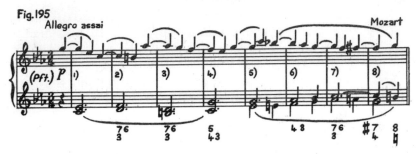

Fig.195

4. The suspended notes in Fig. 195 create three different sets of circumstances:

A.

5. The melody notes tied over into bars 1 and 5 are consonant with the new chord and, on this account, are free to move by step or leap in any direction. The first two beats of these particular bars do not, therefore, show us anything we have not come across in earlier chapters.

B.

6. The notes tied over into bars 2, 3, 4, 6, and 7 are *dissonant* with the new chord on the first beat, and all descend one step to become consonant. All the tied notes of this group are called ' suspensions '. A ' suspension ' (as appears from these five examples) is a melodic progression in three stages:

> (*i*)   the ' preparation ': the sounding of a harmony note on a previous weak beat;

> (*ii*)   the ' suspension ' proper: which is dissonant with the bass of the new chord and occurs on a *strong* beat;

> (*iii*)   the ' resolution ': by which the suspension resolves *downwards* by step on to a harmony note of the new chord.

7. In addition to these three stages, it should be noted that:

> (*iv*)   no suspension can be prepared by a passing note (which, by definition, cannot be a harmony note);

> (*v*)   the note suspended can equally well be a repetition of the preparation and not a tied note: this will often be the case in vocal music where the preparation, suspension, and resolution may be allotted to three syllables—see Fig. 158 in which the tenor (bar 1) and soprano (bar 2) sound a suspension to three different syllables;

> (*vi*)   the preparation will generally occupy not less than one full beat; it should rarely be shorter than the note of suspension to which it is tied; there is more latitude in

this regard when the suspended note is repeated;

(*vii*)   the suspended note will generally be not less than a sub-unit (Chap. 8, paras. 27–31), though it will more frequently be at least one full beat (Fig. 196, (*iv*)–(*vii*));

(*viii*)   the resolution is not restricted as to duration, and may move at once to another harmony note or to a passing note.

8. Fig. 196 illustrates the essentials of simple suspensions: examine this in detail.

Available Suspensions

9. Since suspensions are dependent on the dissonances which exist in diatonic harmony they will be centred on the seventh, the fourth, and the compound interval of the second; that is, the ninth.

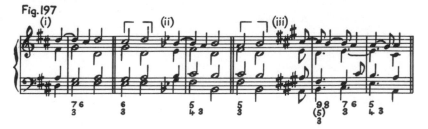

Foundation Chords

10. From Fig. 197 it will be seen (*i*) that on resolving 7 to 6 the chord (the foundation chord) is $\frac{6}{3}$; (*ii*) that, on resolving 4 to 3, the foundation chord is $\frac{5}{3}$; and (*iii*) that the progression 9 8 is basically a triad in root position—that is, the foundation chord is $\frac{5}{3}$. (It is rare to find the suspension 2 1 and, for that reason, its existence will be ignored in the present volume. Fig. 198 contains a true 2 1 suspension; but we shall do well to avoid such rarities for the moment.)

Fig.198   Palestrina

po-ten — ti — — am   in

3
2   1   5
        4   3

11. The approach to the foundation chord of a suspension differs in no way from the approach to the same chord when it lacks a suspension.

Suspensions in the Bass

12. Para. 6 (*ii*) stated that the note of suspension is dissonant with the bass. The exception is when the suspension itself is in the bass. In such cases the suspended note, instead of being pulled downwards by the bass, is forced downwards by the dissonance above it: the only interval which can create this dissonance is the second. Suspensions in the bass are not as common as in middle or upper parts, yet they need not be avoided. In two-part writing they have a useful function since they can alternate with suspensions in the upper part or ornament cadences.

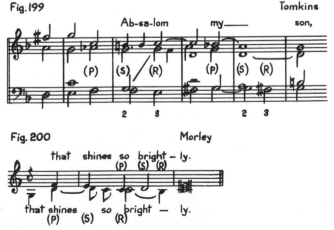

Fig.199   Tomkins

Ab-sa-lom   my____   son,

(P) (S) / (R)   (P) (S) (R)

2   3   2   3

Fig. 200   Morley

that   shines   so   bright – ly.
                 (P) (S) (R)

that shines   (S)   so bright — ly.
(P)   (R)

Doubling

13. The problem of doubling in four-part harmony affects principally the chord sounded at the moment of suspension: that is, the strong beat.

14. We cannot double the suspended note itself, since it is a

discord and must fall by step. The remaining notes in the foundation chord of a suspension may follow the normal principles for doubling. Thus, in the progression $\frac{7}{3}$ ^{6}, the third will be doubled rather than the bass: in $\frac{5}{4}$ $_3$, either the root or the fifth: in $\frac{9}{3}$ ^{8} there is less need to double any note as there are already three available to sustain the suspension, but if the part-writing demands a doubled note, double the root and omit the fifth. (Fig. 197)

C.

15. We will discuss suspensions again later in this chapter. Meanwhile, referring once more to Fig. 195, you will see that in bar 8 there is not only a suspension in the middle voice—C falling to B♮—but also a tied note in the soprano part which resolves *upwards*—F♯ rising to G. The latter is an upward suspension or, as it is sometimes called, a retardation. While the term 'retardation' may appear somewhat illogical (for is not every suspension the retardation of at least one note?) it does help to distinguish between a suspension which resolves downwards, and one which resolves upwards.

16. A retardation is less common than a downward suspension. It can form part of the ornamentation of authentic or interrupted cadences, the leading note being tied over before stepping upwards to the tonic. As in the instance in Fig. 195, a retardation is sometimes combined with an ordinary suspension.

Fig.201   (Adagio)   Bach

The Placing of Suspensions

17. We know already that if a given note is tied over to a strong beat and then falls by step, there may be an opportunity for sounding a suspension. (It is more difficult to remember that a *dotted note* can be the same as a tied note in this connection). We know also that the moment of suspension (that is, of discord) must be on a strong beat and the resolution on a weaker beat. But confusion sometimes arises as to the *relative weakness* of beats in a bar (Chap. 8, paras. 26–31). For example, in $\frac{4}{4}$ or C at *allegro*, the even beats

will be weak: so the second beat is the earliest moment for resolving a suspension sounded on the first; and the fourth for a suspension sounded on the third beat (Fig. 202 (*i*)). But since resolutions may be delayed, the third beat can, equally, be the point of resolution for a suspension sounded on the *first* beat; or the first for one sounded on the third beat of the previous bar. Thus, while the first and third beats can be regarded as strong *or* weak (in relation to each other), they are both strong in relation to the second and fourth.

Fig. 202

18. Only in exceptional circumstances should the *even* beats in duple time at a fairly fast pace be regarded as strong enough to support the discordant moment of a suspension (Fig. 208). At present you should avoid placing a suspension on weak beats of the bar.

19. In triple time at *allegro*, the first and second beats can be points of suspension; but *not* the third beat (Chap. 8, para. 29). The resolution may either be on a succeeding beat in the same bar, or be postponed until the first beat of the following bar.

Fig. 203

20. If the *tempo* be slower (*andante* or *adagio*), a resolution in simple time may well be sounded a half-beat (instead of a whole beat) after the suspension. The even beats (and the third in triple time) may be 'strong' enough to carry a suspension: but care is needed.

Fig. 204

21. In compound time the beats are best reckoned as dotted units: but if the *tempo* is not too fast, suspensions can be resolved on the sub-units of the chief beats (Chap. 8, para. 31).

Fig. 205

Suspensions in Cadences

22. In many styles of music it is customary to include a suspension in the cadential approach to the final chord of a phrase or movement (Figs. 185, 187, 189, etc.). We have already seen that a suspension may also be sounded with the final chord itself and resolved as it is sustained (Figs. 195 and 201): but while this is often suitable in the middle of a movement (to maintain the rhythm), it is comparatively rare in the writings of the great composers at movement-endings: follow their example by not introducing it too frequently in this context.

Exercises

(In the exercises in this chapter only *one* suspension should be sounded at any one moment).

1. Rewrite the following passages so as to include such suspensions and retardations as are (musically) possible.

Ex. 1

Movement during Resolution

23. It is not essential for the free voices to remain stationary while a suspension is being resolved. They can either move to other notes of the foundation chord (see the soprano in Fig. 206); or the foundation chord itself can be changed as the note of resolution is sounded (Fig. 207). In the latter case the figuring will be misleading because of the movement of the bass: 7 will not be followed (in the figures) by a 6; nor 4 by a 3. (An extreme instance of chords changing in conjunction with suspensions is the sequence at Fig. 208; do not imitate this at present.)

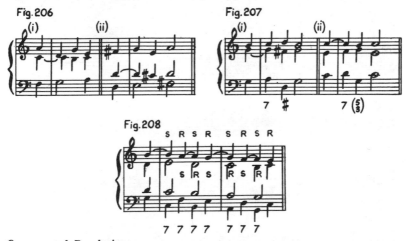

Ornamental Resolutions

24. In all resolutions shown so far the suspended note has fallen one degree by step. Yet frequently it will not move directly to the resolution. Instead it will either move first to another harmony note of the foundation chord, or sound some note-pattern which will include the note of resolution.

25. First, the movement to another harmony note of the foundation chord. It will be seen in Fig. 209 that the harmony note can

either be above or below the suspended note. Passing notes and auxiliaries can also be included (Fig. 210). It is unwise to treat suspensions in the bass in the same manner.

Fig. 209

Fig. 210

26. The note-patterns referred to in para. 24 are many: they usually include (*i*) a fall of a third before rising to the note of resolution; or (*ii*) a rise of one degree before falling to the note of resolution (Fig. 211). Very often such patterns are still further embellished, as at (*iii*) and (*iv*) below.

Fig. 211

27. The fall of a third (as at *) may create a discord with the bass. This is ignored, being on a weak beat; just as a discord produced by an unaccented passing note is ignored.

28. A retardation may also be embellished: usually by a leap

upwards of a third before settling on the note of resolution (Fig. 212).

29. Decorative additions to suspensions and retardations may cause forbidden consecutives. For the present, restrict yourself to using simple patterns: the following are recommended. (That at (*iii*) below employs an anticipating note.[1])

Exercises

2. Rewrite the exercises in Question 1, adding simple decoration to the suspensions.

3. Add parts for alto and tenor, and introduce suspensions to fit the given figuring.

---

[1] See Chapter 22.

4. Add three parts above, and introduce some suspensions.

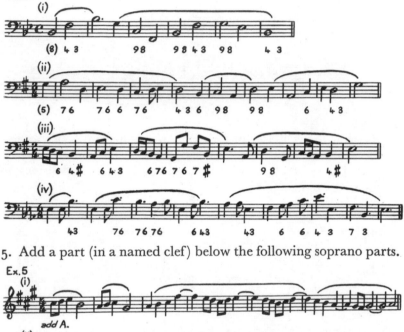

5. Add a part (in a named clef) below the following soprano parts.

6. Add a part (in a named clef) above the following.

Ex.6

7. Sing the following exercise and note the movement of the parts during the preparation, sounding and resolution of the suspensions.

Ex.7 Allegretto

Take five pounds of brains of your Jan-u'-ry flies, And for-ty true

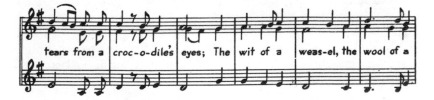

tears from a croc-o-dile's eyes; The wit of a weas-el, the wool of a

frog, With an / With an   ounce of con-serve, of   Mich-ael-mas   fog.

8. Write down given passages from dictation.

16. APPOGGIATURAS AND ACCIACCATURAS

1. Much confusion arises in writing and interpreting these two terms. In a study of harmony we are concerned only with the appoggiatura: the acciaccatura is only mentioned to ensure that the distinction is clear.

The Acciaccatura

2. The acciaccatura, literally a ' crushing ' note, is an ornament to be found (strictly) only in keyboard music of not later date than the mid-eighteenth century. In playing an essential note, the note next below or above it is struck at the same moment *and released immediately*. This device is usually indicated by writing the acciaccatura itself in small type and adding an oblique stroke across the stem.

Fig. 214

sounded:-

3. The acciaccatura is discordant: it is an unessential note. No attempt is made to resolve it (as we did the suspension). It is struck *on* the beat with the note it adorns.

4. String and wind instruments made attempts to imitate the acciaccatura by playing the unessential note on the beat and moving very quickly to the harmony note to which it belonged. This false form of acciaccatura was later widely adopted in piano music, though in such cases it ceases to be a ' crushing ' note and becomes a ' leaning ' note, or short appoggiatura (Figs. 215 and 216). You need not worry unduly about it, except to remember that the unessential note is played on the beat and is written with a stroke across the stem.

Fig. 215

Fig. 216

The Appoggiatura

5. This ornament, literally a 'leaning' note, is also an unessential note which moves one step up or down to an essential note: yet it differs from the true acciaccatura. The appoggiatura is not restricted to keyboard instruments: it can equally well appear in a voice part or in a passage for strings or woodwind. It is not played simultaneously with its principal note: but, being sounded before it *on the beat*, diminishes the duration of the principal note by its own length. It is usually printed in smaller type, but should have no oblique stroke through the stem.

Fig. 217

6. There are several forms of the appoggiatura: and its use has varied at different times in musical history. At present you need only know its basic form and how it differs (as an ornament) from the acciaccatura.

The Appoggiatura in Harmony and Melody

7. Just as it is possible to write a suspension with a repeated note (as at (i) below), so it is possible to write the foundation chord of the same progressions on the accented beat and to include the suspended notes as appoggiaturas (Fig. 218 (ii)).

Fig. 218

8. The examples above show that the accented non-harmony notes of a suspension can, if we like, be written out and analysed as appoggiaturas. This interpretation can also be applied to other progressions: for instance, we can re-write Figs. 44 and 45 in the same manner.

Fig. 219

9. The appoggiatura is important to us here not as a pure ornament but rather as an interpretation of many points in melodies whose harmonic explanation is otherwise less clear. In Fig. 218 it was shown that a suspension can be interpreted as a note leaning towards the foundation chord. The cadential six-four is also an appoggiatura leaning to the $\frac{5}{3}$ on the dominant (Fig. 219). And we shall come across many other progressions which can be explained in a similar manner. Thus, the simple phrase at Fig. 220 is to be found ornamented by appoggiaturas in a piano sonata by Mozart (Fig. 221). Compare these two examples carefully: examine the figuring of the appoggiaturas in bar 3 of the latter and you will find that the first quaver of each beat is dissonant and leans on to the second quaver, which is the essential note.

Fig. 220

Fig. 221

Allegretto grazioso   Mozart

p

10. In the third bar of Fig. 221 we have a simple progression ornamented by appoggiaturas. This is quite clear. You may then ask if, on being given those eight quavers to harmonize, it is wrong to set a different chord against each one. There are two answers. First, it is not wrong *if* the sounding of eight chords instead of four is satisfactory to the ear and is the effect you want: second, it is wrong if you are trying to imitate the style of Mozart or Haydn. Compare Mozart's version of this bár with the two harmonizations below. Do all three sound right? Do they all have the same character and feeling? You must answer these questions for yourself.

Fig. 222

Fig. 223

Ⅴ I I Ⅴ Ⅴ$^6_5$I I⁶ Ⅳ

11. Where does the difference lie in these three versions? Is it not in the root progressions? Mozart gives us only four ornamented

chords in that bar: each one beginning with the tension of discord and ending with the consonance of resolution. Fig. 222 is colourless and fussy, because the sequence of thirds and sixths makes the root progression ambiguous. You will consider Fig. 223 (it is hoped) awkward and, again, fussy: it is a thoroughly bad example of harmonization as it calls for the rapid sounding of eight chords, all based on primary roots.

12. This comparison suggests that Mozart's version is the best. It also shows that, just as we can reduce the number of new chords in a bar by treating certain notes as unaccented passing notes, so our root progressions may be simplified and the musical value of our harmonizations increased if we treat suitable notes as appoggiaturas. Of course, there may be no such opportunity in a given phrase: but if you see two adjacent notes lying one step apart, look at them carefully and decide if they can suitably be treated as an appoggiatura moving to its essential note. In doing this, remember that

(*i*)   an unaccented passing note is unstressed and is always approached and quitted by step;

(*ii*)   a suspension receives a stress and is always approached from the same note and quitted (in its simplest shape) by step; and

(*iii*) an appoggiatura receives a stress and is approached by leap or by step and is quitted by step.

Exercises

1. Mark the appoggiaturas in the following passages. Write out their foundation chords and add Roman numerals.

Ex.1

(i)

(ii)   Mozart

2. Rewrite the following passages with appoggiaturas or suspensions in suitable places.

Ex.2

3. Complete these cadences. Include some appoggiaturas in the soprano part.

Ex.3

4. Add three parts below.

Ex.4

5. Add a second part below.

6. Write down given passages from dictation.

17. TRIADS IN THE SECOND INVERSION

1. It was said in Chapter 5 that the second inversion of the common chord, or six-four, is a chord in its own right. It has its own characteristics, its own colour. And it calls for careful handling, especially in approaching and quitting its bass note.

2. One feature which distinguishes the six-four from the other positions of the triad is that all the notes of the chord must be sounded. Neither the sixth nor the fourth can be omitted without creating

ambiguity. An exception is in two-part writing, when the six-four can be implied by broken chords (that is, by subsidiary harmony notes): a sixth alone on the dominant is sometimes sufficient to suggest the well-known cadential pattern which uses the second inversion *on* the dominant.

Fig. 224

3. A further feature of the second inversion of the triad is that the dissonant fourth is usually unprepared—that is, it is treated as an appoggiatura: though it can be prepared if circumstances demand it. Its resolution will be considered in paras. 6-20.

Doubling

4. The fourth, being dissonant, should not be doubled (but see also para. 8 below). The bass, preferably, or the sixth can be doubled with good effect.

Fig. 225

Uses of the Six-four

5. Compared with the root position and first inversion of the triad, the second inversion is used sparingly. Its principal function is to embellish a phrase, or to link two chords. These functions can best be considered under three headings:

> the cadential six-four;
> the auxiliary six-four; and
> the passing six-four.

The Cadential Six-four

6. This has already been referred to in Chapter 5. It is part of one of the most common of all cadential patterns. The second inversion *on* the dominant resolves on to the root position *of* the dominant

triad in preparation for the tonic or (in an interrupted cadence)
VI.

Fig.226

c I⁶₄ V I   c I⁶₄ V♮ VI

7. In quitting the cadential six-four the bass remains still: the
dissonant fourth is resolved on to the third below: and the sixth,
in falling to the fifth, either moves simultaneously with the fourth;
or moves first, thus creating a suspension (see (*ii*) below). The
fourth should rarely fall before the sixth in a major cadence(and
more rarely still in the minor) as the effect is weak. (See para. 13.)

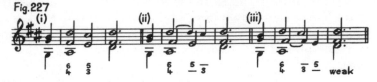

Fig.227

8. Should the movement of the parts make it necessary to double
the fourth, one of the two must leap to another harmony note
while the six-four is being sounded or rise to some note of the next
chord: the other fourth will resolve downwards by step in the
normal manner.

Fig.228

The conditions in Fig. 228 are not common. Do not make
strenuous efforts to double the fourth in the six-four.

9. The six-four should receive a stronger accent than its resolution.
Its duration may be longer or shorter than the resolution; or be
equal to it. The six-four itself is sometimes embellished with an
auxiliary note (or notes); with some pattern such as is used in
resolving suspensions; or with an additional (but unaccented)
chord, such as II⁶, before V. (In the latter case the bass will move:
see also para. 18.)

Fig. 229

I$^6_4$ II*V

10. It is on a six-four on the dominant that the orchestra, in the classical concerto, pauses before the soloist plays an elaborate cadential resolution (or *cadenza*). The movement is resumed as the soloist resolves the dominant chord on to the tonic.

Bass Movement

11. The approach to the bass of the cadential six-four may safely be by step. II^6 and IV are possible if the bass is to rise; VI and IV^6 if it is to fall (Fig. 225). To these may be added I, II and I^6 (but *not* III) as approaches to I$^6_4$, in which cases the bass will leap to the six-four. All are equally good in either major or minor keys.

12. The character of the six-four as an appoggiatura is very marked when used in the imperfect cadence (Fig. 66).

13. At this point we may refer to the augmented triad (Chap. 14, para. 7) which, in its first inversion (on the dominant), may be described as an appoggiatura to the cadential six-four. A famous example is to be found in Orlando Gibbons's madrigal ' The Silver Swan ' (Fig. 230). Here the B♮ is the appoggiatura and carries the principal accent of the progression. The first inversion of the augmented triad, you will see, is consonant but requires resolution by raising the sharpened third to the fourth. In this context it can only be used in a *minor* cadence.

Fig. 230   Gibbons

breast   a — gainst the reed-y   shore

— gainst the reed — y   shore,   Thus
                             ♭6   —   5   —
                             ♮   4   ♮

The Auxiliary Six-four

14. This is simply the decoration of a triad by raising the third and fifth one degree and lowering them again (Fig. 231). In its structure it differs in no way from an auxiliary note. An auxiliary six-four is usually unaccented; but it is frequently to be found

K

bearing a varying amount of accentuation (Figs. 232 and 233).

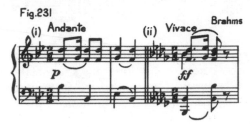

15. There is no movement of the bass during the sounding of an auxiliary six-four.

16. It can only be included in two-part writing when broken chords outline the complete chord.

The Passing Six-four

17. This exists in two forms. As an approach to a cadence. And as a link between the root position and first inversion of certain triads. Neither form has any place in two-part writing.

18. When used in approaching a cadence, the cadential six-four is shifted one beat further from the cadence (to a weak or weaker beat) to make room for a first inversion of the 7th on the supertonic (Chap. 21) before V. In this context the six-four loses much of its cadential character; hence the reference to it here as a passing six-four.

19. There are many similar instances of this progression in Bach's harmonizations of chorales. Note that the bass of the six-four is approached by step from above and proceeds to the subdominant: and that its octave moves by step in contrary motion.

20. As a link the six-four is subject to considerable restrictions. Thus, it can only link the root position and first inversion (respectively) of I, II (but not in the minor), IV and VI. In all instances either position can precede the other. The bass of the six-four should be doubled in the top part, and both these parts should move by step in contrary motion to one another. The only latitude permitted is that the passing six-four may fall either on an accented or on an unaccented beat.

21. The functions of the six-four described in this chapter are sufficient for present needs. Except where stated, they are applicable to both major and minor keys. Try to understand this chord and do not hesitate to use it in a suitable context. On the other hand, beware of the six-four which cannot readily be analysed as falling under one of the headings given above.

Exercises

1. Write out the possible approaches to the bass of a six-four. Figure with Roman numerals.

2. Add three parts below. Use a six-four where marked in the first three exercises: in the remaining ones, make your own choice as to where this chord should be introduced. The number of

times a six-four can suitably be introduced in each exercise is given in brackets.

Ex.2

3. Add three parts above.

Ex.3

4. Add one part below.

Ex.4

5. Add one part above. The number of six-fours which can suitably be implied is given in brackets.

Ex.5

6. Extemporize at the piano short phrases (four or five chords each) in named keys. Each one should end with either an authentic or an imperfect cadence, and should include a six-four chord.

7. Explain why the augmented triad can only precede a six-four in a minor cadence. Write out an example in a named key.

8. Write down given passages from dictation.

18. SIMPLE MODULATION IN FOUR PARTS

1. In Chapter 1 we saw that a new scale can be built on the upper tetrachord of C major if an F sharp is added to the leading note: and that this new scale is G major. Similarly, a new scale can be built on the lower tetrachord of C major (proceeding downwards) if a B flat is added: this new scale is F major.

2. So an F sharp must be added if a passage of music is to move or, as we say, modulate from C to G major; and, even more important, we must get rid of the F natural which is foreign to G major. To modulate to F major from C major, B flat must be added; and the B natural (an important influence in C major, being the leading note) must be omitted.

Exercises in Modulation

3. To modulate, (*i*) the old key must first be established: (*ii*) some means must be found of undermining the loyalty to the old key and anticipating an adherence to the new: (*iii*) the new key must be established.

4. The first stage can be effected by a few chords which are closely linked to the original key and which will probably include both I and V in root position or first inversion.

5. At the beginning of the second stage an attempt will be made to

find one or more chords which, while belonging to the old key, also belong to the new. That is, on arrival these chords belong to the old key; on departure they have changed their loyalty and belong to the new. Such a chord is often referred to as a 'pivot' chord: the name matters less than the fact that at this point the music begins to shed its connection with the old key and shows the first signs of being established in the new.

Fig. 236

6. Before harmonizing the above melody, we must note that an F sharp in the final cadence shows there has been a modulation from C major to G major (the dominant).

7. The original key can be established in the course of the first two bars. (The chord in brackets reminds us that the tonality is still firmly in C major.)

Fig. 237

C I⁶ IV V⁴³

8. The cadence in G major can also be harmonized without difficulty.

Fig. 238

G I II⁶ V I

9. There remains the third bar, in the course of which the tonality of C major must be undermined, and that of G major prepared. C I, C V, and C IV should be avoided as preserving the old tonality. But C III can become G VI, and C VI can become G II. Can these two chords prepare the way for the primary chords of G major? The following working of this bar shows that this is possible.

Fig.239

C III VI
  G II V⁶ I

10. The three sections can finally be put together. But in doing so some attention should be paid to the rhythm of the finished exercise. The melody itself is given and so cannot be altered. Its rhythm is not altogether satisfactory. Can the addition of passing notes in the lower parts improve matters? Here your judgement, as the composer, is all-important. Below is given the rhythm of the melody as it stands, together with an over-all rhythm which might be regarded as an improvement.

Fig.240

melody:-

suggested over-all rhythm

11. Without much difficulty this rhythm can be introduced by adding passing notes. The finished result will then be as follows:

Fig.241

C I II⁶ V   I⁶ IV V⁴³   III VI   II⁶ V I
                         G II V⁶ I

12. A modulation from C major to F major (the subdominant) can be made in a similar way. First, the melody.

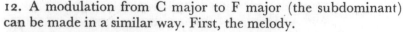

Fig.242

13. Now the first phrase (with the existing tonic chord in brackets):
and then the cadence in the new key.

Fig. 243

C IV I⁶I II⁶ I⁶₄V   F IV I⁶ IV V I

14. The pivot chord in this instance is C I which is changed (in
the composer's mind) to F V; after which the essential B flat is
introduced by F VII⁶.

Fig. 244

C V I I
F V VII⁶ I VI

15. The rhythm needs, perhaps, only three slight modifications:
two to the bass line, and one to the alto. And the finished passage
can then be written out complete.

Fig. 245

melody:-

suggested
over-all rhythm

Fig. 246

C IV VI   IV I⁶I II⁶   I⁶₄V V   I I
                              F V VII⁶I VI   IV I⁶ IV V   I

Related Keys

16. The modulations in this chapter have so far been made to the dominant and subdominant. Both these keys are said to be related to the tonic because of the notes common to the respective scales, and the triads common to the two keys. Thus, seven notes in G major are shared with C major: and a different seven notes of F major with C major. There are also four triads common to both G and C major:

$$\left\{\begin{array}{llll} G & I, & II, & IV & \text{and} & VI \\ C & V, & VI, & I & \text{and} & III \end{array}\right.$$

and four triads common to F and C major:

$$\left\{\begin{array}{llll} F & I, & III, & V, & VI \\ C & IV, & VI, & I, & II \end{array}\right.$$

17. There are three other keys which are said to be ' related ' to the tonic, whether it be major or minor: the relative minor (or major) of the tonic—which shares the same key-signature; the relative of the dominant; and the relative of the subdominant. These give any tonic *five* nearly related keys. If we turn to Fig. 58 we can see that any tonic is the centre of a sector of the key cycle, and that its five related keys lie facing it and immediately on either hand. Thus:

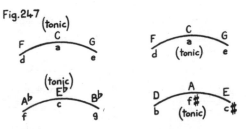

Fig. 247

18. Keys which are not related—that is, which are dissonant with a tonic—are said to be unrelated or (in certain instances) remote.

Modulations from a Minor Key

19. The two most important modulations when the tonic is in the minor are to the relative major and the dominant minor: both of these are related keys. The relative major, sharing the same key-signature, stands in much the same relation to a minor key as the dominant to a major one. Compositions in the major usually include a modulation to, and an important cadence in, the dominant: contrast in a piece whose tonic is in the minor will often be found in the relative major (see para. 26 (*vi*)).

20. It was shown in Chapter 14, para. 4 that unless the minor key is continually re-affirmed (by raising the leading note and, perhaps, the sixth degree as well) the tonality will easily slide into that of the relative major (Fig. 186). So we can modulate to the relative major by omitting reference to the *ascending* melodic scale, and by treating the flattened leading note as the dominant of the new key.

Fig.248

f♯   I I⁶ IV
        A II V V⁶ I

In Fig. 248 the key of F sharp minor is not abandoned until (in bar 2) IV is quitted as the supertonic of A major. After that the new key is established in the normal way.

21. In moving to the dominant minor, the sixth of the old key must be sharpened to become the supertonic of the new: and the leading note of the old key should be flattened during the transition, or else we shall have a strong feeling that the new key is not established but is only acting as the dominant of the old (bar 4 of Fig. 249).

Fig.249

c I   I⁶ II⁶ V♮   V⁶ I I⁶
                g IV⁶ V♯ I I⁶ IV I⁶   V♯ I

Exercises

These exercises modulate from the major to the dominant or subdominant; and from the minor to the relative major or dominant minor. The pivot chord is marked (+). Later you will have to work your modulations unaided in this respect. Harmonize the establishment of the old key and then the final cadence (if you wish) before considering the pivot chords. Write the basic chords in ink and add melodic or rhythmic decoration in pencil.

1. Add parts for alto and tenor.

Ex.1

(i) g-Bb

(ii) Db-Ab

(iii) G-C

(iv) d-a

(v) e-b

(vi) d-F

2. Add three parts below.

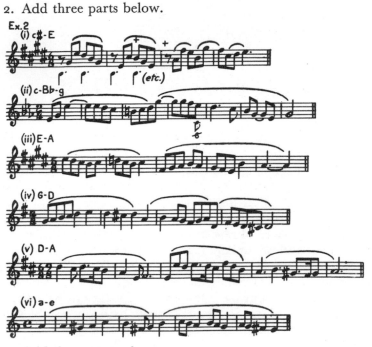

3. Add three parts above.

Establishing a Key

22. In Figs. 241 and 246 the root position of the new key is sounded some beats before the final cadence (*). If these passages are played from the beginning as far as the asterisk it will be realised that no satisfactory termination has been reached: there is no sense of being securely in the new key. Now, it requires *at least* two chords to establish a key, but very often the context will demand an even longer phrase to do this. For this reason, before the final cadence additional chords are sounded which may well include the subdominant *in the bass*, or II, II⁶, IV or VI. In Fig. 249 no modulation to G minor has been 'established' by the time we reach the asterisk: but the addition of a cadence in which the subdominant steps upwards to the cadential six-four establishes the new tonality without doubt.

Transient Modulations

23. It is not always desirable or necessary to establish a new key too firmly: very often it is sufficient to suggest a fresh tonality in passing—there being no intention to stay in it. This is called a transient modulation. As the name implies, it appears in the course of a passage and never at the end. (An interrupted cadence is not a transient modulation—though it can, and sometimes does, introduce a substantive modulation.)

Key Sequence

24. In the exercises given so far in this chapter the modulations are named or determined. Later, when writing and harmonizing melodies, you will have to choose the key or keys which must be established or suggested.

25. The choice of keys is not haphazard. Examination of well-established songs as well as compositions by the great composers will show that it is usual to move reasonably direct to the dominant (if the original tonic is major) and to the dominant or relative major (if the original tonic is minor); and then to touch on other related keys before returning to the original tonic (para. 22 above). Typical key sequences are sketched briefly in Figs. 250 and 251.

Fig. 250
Allegretto

Fig. 251
Andante

26. The choice of keys lies with the composer, but the establishment of the tonic and the return (often via the subdominant) are
important features which have received recognition almost
universally. You can with profit refer to the following works,
whose key sequence can be outlined as follows:

    (*i*)   Come Lasses and Lads. (C major)
         bar 1, C: 4, C: 5, a: 8, a: 10, CIV: 12, CV: 13, C:
         16, CV: 17, C: 19, CIV, I, V: 20, C
    (*ii*) Heart of Oak. (A major)
         bar 1, A: 4, cad. in A: 8, cad. in E: 10, A: 11, f♯: 12, A:
         13, AIV, I: 14, V, I

(*iii*) The Oak and the Ash. (f minor)
bar 1, f: 4, fV: 5, A♭: 8, fV: 9, A♭: 11, fI, V: 12, plagal
cad. in f

(*iv*) ' Aberystwyth '. (e minor)
bar 1, e: 2, cad. in e: 4, eI, V♯: 5, e: 6, cad. in e: 8, cad.
in e ‖ 9, C: 10, cad. in G: 11, e: 12, cad. in b: 13, G:
14, cad. in eV: 15, e: 16, cad. in e

(*v*) Beethoven, Symphony No. 2, Larghetto. (A major)
bar 1, A: 4, AV: 5, A: 7–8 cad. in E: ‖: 17–18, A: 19–20,
AV: 23, A II, V: 24, A:‖

(*vi*) Beethoven, Symphony No. 7. Allegretto (a minor)
bar 1, a: 4, a: 5, a: 6, C I$^{6}_{4}$: 7, CV: 8, C ‖: 9–10, B:
11–12, A: 13, a: 15, A I$^{6}_{4}$, V♯: 16, a:‖

(*vii*) Beethoven, ' Emperor ' Piano Concerto, Adagio (B
major)
bar 1, B: 4, BV: 5, BV, I: 6, BV, I: 7, B, g♯: 8, g♯, B:
9, B IV, V$^{6}_{4}$, I, IV: 10, int'pt'd. cad. in B: 11, as 9:
12, cad. in B: 13–16, coda on pedal B

(*viii*) Brahms, Symphony No. 1, Finale (C major)
bar 1, C: 4, CV: 5, C: 8, CV, I: 9, CV: 12, aI, VI:
13–14, CV: 16, C II^{6}, V: 17, C

Exercises

4. Give the names and key-signatures of the five keys nearly
related to D, B♭, F♯, E♭ and B major: and e, g, b, c♯ and f minor.
(In the following exercises, modulate to the keys named.)

5. Add parts for alto and tenor.

Ex.5

(iii) e‑G‑e

(iv) Bb‑g‑c‑Eb‑Bb

6. Add three parts below.

Ex.6

(i) f#‑A‑C#‑f#

(ii) F‑d‑F

IVII

(iii) A-E-c#-f#-A

(iv) g-Bb-g

7. Add three parts above.

Ex.7

(i) C-G-e-a

etc.

(ii) Eb-Ab-f

etc.

(iii) d-g-Bb-d

etc.

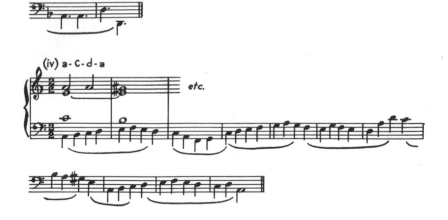

(iv) a-c-d-a

etc.

19. SIMPLE MODULATION IN TWO PARTS

1. In two-part writing the problem is to make clear the choice of chords. This is especially important when modulating. There must be no doubt as to what chord is implied. An uncertain, hazy tonality is unsatisfactory.

2. The method of modulating in two parts is similar to that in four or any other number of parts: find a chord or succession of chords which will dispel the tonality of the old key and establish the new key: support the new key by introducing important notes such as the leading note and subdominant.

3. Broken-chord figures are helpful in tracing the chord- and root-progressions in two parts. There is no difficulty in figuring the passage in Fig. 252 and in tracing the modulation.

Fig.252

4. The A natural of bar 6 is confirmed in bar 7 as the dominant of D. But the A of bar 6 alone is no guarantee of a modulation, for the chord of A major can be the triad on the flattened leading

note of B minor—as Bach shows a few bars earlier in the same Minuet, when he leads to a half-close in the tonic.

Fig. 253

Look carefully at the sixth and seventh bars in these two quotations: write them out as block chords and note the difference between them.

5. The introduction of the leading note of the new key will help to shift the tonality, especially if the modulation is to a key with more sharps, or less flats (that is, moving clockwise on Fig. 58). But the modulation may not be firmly established until additional chords have been implied in the new key. Thus, in Fig. 254, though B flat major is suggested at *, it is not confirmed as a modulation until the cadence at the end of the phrase. (See also Chap. 18, para. 22.)

Fig. 254

6. In moving anti-clockwise in the key cycle (more flats or less sharps) the subdominant of the new key is a powerful factor, especially if combined with the dominant or leading note. A modulation by such means can either be permanent or, provided the new key is not too firmly established, merely temporary. The transient nature of a modulation is helpful when touching the key of the subdominant before closing in the tonic. In Fig. 255, Bach touches on F major for half a bar before re-asserting the leading note (and thereby the tonality) of C.

Fig. 255

C I⁶   I⁶₄ II⁶ I⁶   C IV II⁶¹⁶ V⁵₄³⁷   I
   F V⁶₅ V⁷ VI V⁶₄ I

7. Not all two-part writing can be built on broken chords. Often a search must be made for the most suitable root-progression—as when writing in four parts. The first and last phrases of the melody in Fig. 256 are identical: yet the first can be harmonized as a plagal cadence in F major, and the last as an authentic cadence in C major.

Fig. 256

F   I   C V I   I⁶₄ V I

8. In adding the second part, bear in mind the most suitable number of *harmonies* in a bar (Chap. 8, paras. 33–35). In this melody it will be two; except in bar 3 where the suspension demands three harmonies. Whenever the upper part sustains a dotted crotchet, the rhythm can be maintained by passing notes in the lower voice.

Fig. 257

9. Once the harmonization has been sketched in, the lower part can (in this case) be made more interesting by introducing two suspensions.

Fig. 258

10. Take care never to leave the tonality ambiguous in two-part writing: particularly in approaching cadences which are to confirm a modulation. The establishment of a new key justifies the

occasional use of passing notes which may imply VII (the triad with the diminished fifth) or, to put it differently, the combination of the leading note and subdominant. This is a dissonant interval but it can safely be introduced on an unaccented beat provided the leading note rises by step and the subdominant falls to the third of the tonic chord which follows (Fig. 259). As you gain confidence, so you can decorate simple passages with passing notes, subsidiary harmony notes and ornamental resolutions to suspensions. But do not over-do this: it is better to be simple and clear, than fussy.

Fig. 259

Fig. 260

Exercises

Analyse the modulations in these exercises, preferably *after* you have completed your writing.

1. Add a second part below.

Ex. I

2. Add a second part above.

Ex.2

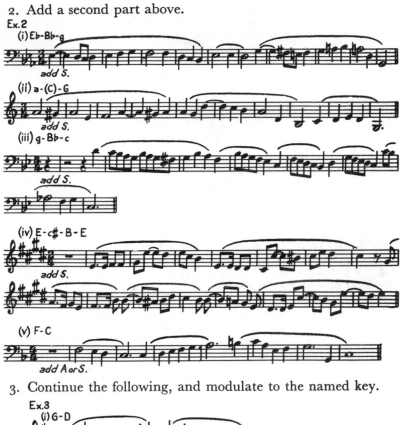

(i) Eb-Bb-g

add S.

(ii) a-(C)-G

add S.

(iii) g-Bb-c

add S.

(iv) E-c#-B-E

add S.

(v) F-C

add A or S.

3. Continue the following, and modulate to the named key.

Ex.3

(i) G-D

(ii) b-D

(iii) Ab-f

(iv) g-Bb

(v) e - G

(vi) A - E

4. Write out the melodies in Exercise 1 above in a named (different) key and add a second part at the piano.

20. THE CHORDS OF THE DOMINANT SEVENTH AND SUPERTONIC SEVENTH
(Root Position)

1. We have now discussed the triads on all degrees of the scale, both major and minor, and their inversions. We built a triad by placing a third and a fifth on a single note. We can form a new series of chords by placing another third on each triad or, in other words, by adding a seventh from the bass. This seventh will in each case follow the key-signature of the diatonic major scale.

Fig. 261

C I^7 II^7 III^7 IV^7 V^7 VI^7 VII^7

2. The notes of each of these chords are a seventh, a fifth, and a third from the bass. But unless the fifth or third is to be altered chromatically, or there is a reason to refer to them specially, these chords are figured 7.

3. Of these chords of the seventh, only those on the dominant and the supertonic will be discussed in this chapter: the remainder we will leave until Book II of this course.

The Dominant Seventh (Root Position)

4. It can be seen from Fig. 261 that this chord is composed of the dominant triad (a major third and a perfect fifth) and a note a

minor seventh from the root. This chord is therefore dissonant. But there is not only a discord between the bass and the seventh: there is also a diminished fifth between the third and the seventh— the outside notes of the triad on VII which we first met in Chapter 5, para. 8, and as recently as Chapter 19, para. 10.

Fig. 262

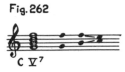

5. These two discords govern to a considerable extent the resolution of this chord. From Fig. 35 we have seen that in VII the subdominant generally falls by step, and the leading note rises. The same movement takes place in the dominant seventh, the seventh falling and the third rising. The fifth is more free. And the bass will leap to the tonic, move by step to the submediant, or remain stationary while V^7 resolves on to I^6_4 for a cadence.

Fig. 263

6. If the fifth is included in both V^7 and I consecutives will appear. To avoid this we must omit the fifth from one of these chords. Thus, at (l) above the fifth is absent from V^7 and present in I: at (m) the fifth does not appear in the final chord but is part of the chord which precedes it. This is a rule and should be observed: but it applies only when both these chords are in root position.

7. The seventh may, if the part-writing allows, step one degree upwards or fall a third before sounding the note of resolution (Fig. 263 (n) and (o)). This agrees with what was said in Chapter 15, para. 26.

Omissions

8. It is common to sound all four notes of the dominant seventh in the same chord. If a note has to be omitted in four-part writing, let it be the fifth—in which case the root should be doubled. In three-part writing it is preferable to omit the fifth, but the third may be omitted if the context is clear.

Doubling

9. The root is the best note to double. The third should not be
doubled, for obvious reasons. It is generally held that the seventh
also should not be doubled, as it is a feature of this chord that this
note should fall. You should follow this recommendation.

Approach

10. Sevenths above the dominant occurred in music before the
time when the chord of the dominant seventh came into general
use. But these sevenths were introduced either as suspensions
(with a preparation, suspension and resolution in the proper
manner) or as passing notes. An example of each is quoted in
Fig. 264.

Fig. 264.   Gibbons

now live, more fools than wise.

It was not until the 17th century that the dominant seventh began
to be used as an unprepared discord. There will be many instances
in which you will be quite correct in using V⁷ unprepared: for
instance, the seventh cannot be prepared if the approach chord is
I, V, or VI. Yet the preparation of the seventh, if the context
allows it, makes for smoothness in part-writing and grace in
style. Approach chords which are likely to permit preparation are
II, II⁶, IV, and IV⁶. (VII⁶ is unsatisfactory because three notes
of V⁷ are already sounding.)

Exercises

1. Add parts for alto and tenor. Introduce V⁷ where suitable.

Ex. I
(i)

(ii)

2. Add three parts below.

The Supertonic Seventh (Root Position)

11. This chord is formed from the triad on the supertonic (a minor third and a perfect fifth) and a note a *minor* seventh from the root. The seventh is the tonic note of the key. It is important to remember the relationship of the root and the seventh to the degrees of the scale.

12. In a major key the seventh alone in II⁷ is dissonant: in a minor key the fifth is also dissonant.

Fig. 265

13. In quitting this chord, the bass may leap to the dominant to become the bass of V or I⁶₄, or it may move to the bass of I⁶ or III. The seventh will fall by step to the leading note—unless II⁷ moves to I⁶, or I⁶₄ (Fig. 266, (*iii*) and (*iv*)). To avoid doubling the third of the dominant triad, the fifth of II⁷ will also fall. The third is free (but see para. 14).

$$\text{II}^7\ \underline{\text{V}} \qquad \text{II}^7\ \underline{\text{V}} \qquad \text{II}^7\ \text{I}^6 \qquad \text{II}^7\ \text{I}^6_4$$

14. An important function of the supertonic seventh (and the reason for referring to it at this point) is as an approach chord to the dominant in preparation for a cadence (Fig. 107). In such a progression the third of II^7 will become the seventh of V^7, thus adding another approach chord to those given in para. 10 above. Look at Fig. 267 and then compare it with Fig. 147: the version with II^7 and V^7 has a richer effect.

Fig. 267

$$\text{II}^7\text{V}^7$$

15. The supertonic seventh in root position can also be used in a minor key. The effect is less satisfactory than in the major owing to the diminished fifth from the bass. We shall see in Chapter 21 that an inversion of II^7 is often a better choice.

Fig. 268

$$\text{D} \qquad \text{II}^7 \qquad\qquad \text{d}\ \ \text{II}^7$$

16. As in the dominant seventh, so in II^7 the seventh itself was originally introduced by preparation, suspension, and resolution. But, while V^7 soon became an unprepared discord, the seventh on the supertonic continued for nearly two centuries to be properly prepared. You also should prepare this seventh whenever possible.

Fig. 269 Philips

Al – le – lu – ia, Al – le – lu – ia.

Exercises

3. Add parts for alto and tenor.

Ex. 3

(i) (ii)

(iii) (iv)

(v)

4. Add three parts above.

Ex. 4

(i) (ii)

(iii) (iv)

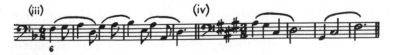

(v)

Modulations

17. The exercises in modulation in Chapters 18 and 19 were worked without the dominant seventh. We had to establish our new key by a series of chords that built up and secured the tonality we wanted. The importance of the dominant seventh is that it establishes a key without doubt when it is followed by the tonic chord. The dominant triad, with its strong root and the leading note, points unmistakably towards the tonic: but when the seventh above the dominant (the subdominant) is added there is a still stronger force welding the tonality to the tonic. So, by using the dominant seventh we can modulate more surely, and often with fewer chords. Yet do not forget that, in spite of its strength, the dominant seventh can become wearisome to the ear if used indiscriminately. Use your judgement and exercise restraint—have you remembered the warning given in Chap. 13, para. 7?

False Relation

18. If, in the course of a modulation, a note sounded in one chord is chromatically altered in the next, it is best to keep that note in the same part. To have the diatonic note in one part and the chromatically changed note in another may create an unpleasant effect: it is called a false relation. Of the two phrases in Fig. 270, the second is the better for your present use. The first is not wrong; but it is reminiscent of a (sixteenth-century) style which is unsuitable for the modulations we are now practising. A parallel example, with the explanation, appears in Fig. 521 in Book II.

Fig. 270

19. The exercises below are devoted to modulations to the five nearly related keys. They are short: but try to make the transition from one key to the other as smooth as possible: and be sure that the new key is firmly established. Do not attempt too elaborate a style of writing: passing notes and suspensions help to make the music interesting, but do not hide the basic progressions by writing too many notes. These two examples are suggestions as to the style you might well adopt in your present work.

Fig. 271

Eb - C minor

EbI VII⁷⁶ II I⁶
c III⁶V⁷VI IVV⁷

Fig. 272

E minor - G major

e I IV I⁶₄ V⁷#VIIV
G II V⁷ VI II⁷V⁷I

Exercises

5. On what degrees of the scale do the roots and sevenths of V⁷ and II⁷ stand? Write down these four notes in the keys of E, Ab, C♯ major: and d, b, and f minor.

6. Write out (and figure) the possible progression of the bass in quitting V⁷ and II⁷.

7. Add parts for alto and tenor.

Ex. 7

(i) Bb - g

(ii) E - B

8. Add three parts below.

Ex.8

9. Add three parts above.

(iv) d-a

10. Add one part below.

Ex.10

(i)

add A.   etc.

(ii)

add A.

(iii)

add B.

(iv)

add T.

11. Add one part above.

Ex. 11

(i)   etc.

add S.

(ii)   etc.

add S.

M

(iii)

(iv) add S.

add S.

12. Write down given passages from dictation.

21. THE DOMINANT SEVENTH AND SUPERTONIC SEVENTH
(Inversions)

1. Just as we found greater freedom in having the inversions of the triads at our disposal, so our part-writing (and particularly the movement of the bass) can gain in flexibility if we make use of the inversions of the dominant and supertonic sevenths.

2. Roman numerals will still be used in this chapter for ease of reference, but you should now try to work your exercises without this aid. The ordinary figured bass will continue to be helpful.

The Inversions of the Dominant Seventh

3. There are three inversions. A sixth is included in each of them. The other intervals should be memorized. It is usual, in figuring these chords, to omit reference to certain intervals: and these are enclosed in brackets in the examples below.

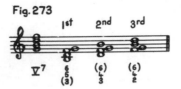

Fig. 273

4. All these inversions are also applicable to the minor keys: the only alteration necessary is the sharpening of the leading note.

First Inversion, $\frac{6}{5}$

5. You can understand this inversion quite simply if you think of it as V⁶ with the subdominant (here a fifth from the bass) added. The bass (the leading note of the key) will rise and the subdominant will fall: the sixth and third are free. The only exception

to the bass rising is when V_5^6 leads to IV^6, in which case the bass will fall and the subdominant will remain stationary.

Fig.274

6. The bass can approach V_5^6 by step upwards or downwards: it can also safely leap downwards (returning within the interval) but should only leap upwards from the supertonic or dominant (Fig. 275).

Fig.275

Exercises

1. Add three parts above. Use V^7 and V_5^6 where suitable.

Ex.1

The Second Inversion, $\frac{4}{3}$

7. It may help if you think of V_3^4 as VII^6 with the dominant note added. Here again, the leading note will rise, but the subdominant (being consonant with the bass in this inversion) is free to *rise or fall* according to the context. The bass will usually rise or fall by step, but reasonable leaps are satisfactory.

8. In a minor key (Fig. (*ii*) above) the figuring must include the sharpened sixth: thus, $\begin{smallmatrix}8\\4\\3\end{smallmatrix}$ ($\begin{smallmatrix}\#6\\4\\3\end{smallmatrix}$) or $\begin{smallmatrix}\natural6\\4\\3\end{smallmatrix}$ (according to the key).

Exercises

2. Add three parts above. Use V^7, V^6_5 and V^4_3 where suitable.

Ex.2
(i)

(ii)

(iii)

The Third Inversion, $\begin{smallmatrix}4\\2\end{smallmatrix}$

9. This inversion is (as it were) composed of V with the sub-dominant added below it. One of its common uses is to lead the harmony from the dominant back to the tonic (Figs. 277 and 278). There is no objection to the sixth rising to double the bass of I^6 (as in Fig. 277). The leading note (the fourth) will rise as usual.

Fig. 277   Haydn

Bb   V V$\frac{4}{2}$I^{6}VII^6

Fig. 278   Wagner

G I^6 V^7 I
         C   V   V$\frac{4}{2}$ I^6

d V$\frac{4}{2}$ I ^{76}

10. You should distinguish between the various positions of the dominant seventh and those of the triad on the leading note. Listen to the difference between the following pairs of chords.

Fig. 279

In your writing you must judge which of these two chords is most suitable. In Fig. 277, Haydn writes the penultimate chord as VII⁶ (not V$_3^4$). In Fig. 291, Handel uses VII⁶ for the fourth quaver of bar 2. Greene, in Fig. 293, writes VII$_3^{76}$ (not V$_4^{76}$) at the beginning of the first full bar, and VII⁶ (with an appoggiatura) in the last chord but one. The absence of the dominant note has a lighter effect. But both chords have their uses and the choice must be made according to the context.

11. As you become accustomed to using the dominant seventh in your own work you will find that the bass line can often be made more smooth by using the first and second inversions in conjunction with I and I⁶. A good example of this is below: note that Mozart chooses VII⁶ (not V$_3^4$) in bar 3.

Fig. 280

Exercises

In these exercises, use V⁷ and the three inversions where suitable.

3. Add three parts below.

Ex. 3

4. Add three parts above.

Ex.4

5. Add a second part below.

Ex.5

add B.

6. Add a second part above.

Ex.6

add S.

7. Write down the following chords on hearing them played on the piano.

Ex.7

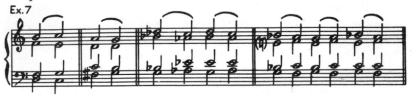

The Inversions of the Supertonic Seventh

12. The supertonic seventh also has three inversions.

Fig.281

13. Since this chord is a useful approach to cadences (Chapter 20, para. 14), one of the important resolutions of these inversions is to a dominant chord or to one of the inversions of the tonic. As in the case of II^7, the seventh from the root is usually prepared—and you should follow this practice whenever possible.

Fig.282   **Philips**

Al – le – lu – ia,   Al – le – lu – ia.

14. The supertonic seventh is a distinguishing feature of many cadences in the chorales harmonized by Bach. The formula most frequently used includes the first inversion. Here also the seventh (that is, the tonic) is prepared. Some typical examples are below. (See also Fig. 182.)

Fig. 283   **Bach**

(i)   (ii)   (iii)

15. It will be remembered that II^6_5 is part of the cadential formula which includes a passing six-four (Fig. 234).

16. II^6_5 (when exchanged for IV) can also give us a highly-coloured variant of the plagal cadence. But it has no part in the cadences generally recognized and should not be indulged in. A well-known quotation in this context is below.

Fig. 284

Largo   Dvorak

17. It is possible to modulate to the nearly related keys by resolving II^7 (or its inversions) on to the dominant seventh or supertonic seventh of the new key. In the examples given in Fig. 285 it is assumed that C major or minor has been established. You should practise modulating to these related keys at the piano and on paper. Begin by using plain chords, and then introduce some decoration by adding passing and auxiliary notes, appoggiaturas and so on.

Fig. 285

C-a   C-F

C-e   C-d   c-Ab

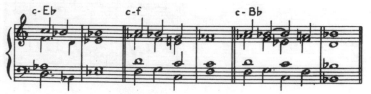

c-Eb   c-f   c-Bb

Exercises

8. Add parts for alto and tenor.

9. Add three parts above.

10. Write down given passages from dictation.

22. ANTICIPATIONS: AND CONCLUSIONS

Anticipations

1. These are simple ornaments which, as the name implies, anticipate the note before which they are sounded. They are the last form of decoration to be introduced in this volume and are important in that they often appear in conjunction with unaccented passing notes, auxiliaries, suspensions, and so on (para. 7 below).

2. Anticipations are unessential notes which may be approached by conjunct or disjunct motion. Being unessential, they will normally create discord, but not always. They most commonly occur in melodic parts, but sometimes in middle parts: they should *not* be used in the bass.

Fig.286   Purcell

(tri) —————— umph sings, (tri) — umph, tri —umph sings,

3. Forbidden consecutives can be created by the inclusion of an anticipating note in an otherwise unobjectionable passage. Fig. 287 is a quotation from Bach: the passing note in the tenor is legitimate, but fifths are created against the soprano because of the anticipation. Do not imitate this progression.

Fig.287   Bach

4. The resolution of a suspension in one part and the sounding of an anticipation in another can create consecutive seconds (Fig. 288). In the quotation from Purcell, the soprano and alto parts proceed logically when considered separately: but when they are laid together two dissonances are sounded. Again, do not imitate this progression in your work at present: remember the existence of this cadence pattern (and its explanation), and note that it is a characteristic of Purcell and the Restoration composers.

Fig.288   Purcell

for | this o – pen | air

5. In music of the 15th and 16th centuries, the resolution of a suspension was commonly decorated with an anticipating note alone. Examples of this are in Figs. 52, 198 and 200.

6. A plain series of notes or chords can come to life by the addition of anticipations. The following progression is the basis of an exquisite passage from Mendelssohn.

Fig.289

Fig.290

Vivace   Mendelssohn

(clar.) f

(str.)   p

And Handel adds interest to a sustained chord by the same method.

Fig.291   Handel

Where e'er you walk   cool gales shall fan the glade.   Trees where you sit

7. But anticipations are most frequently to be found inter-mingled with unaccented passing notes, auxiliary notes, subsidiary harmony notes, suspensions and appoggiaturas. No composer will consciously think of any of these devices; but the analysis of a phrase may well disclose the presence of one or more of them. Thus in Fig. 292, we see an anticipation at (l), appoggiaturas at (m) and (n), a passing note at (o), and a subsidiary harmony note at (p). In Fig. 293, there are appoggiaturas at (l)

and anticipations at (m). The semiquavers marked (p) are, strictly, resolutions of the appoggiaturas which precede them, though the contexts suggest they are anticipations: as a compromise we can say they are both. Study these quotations. Notice the methods by which the semiquaver movement is maintained smoothly and without effort.

Fig.292

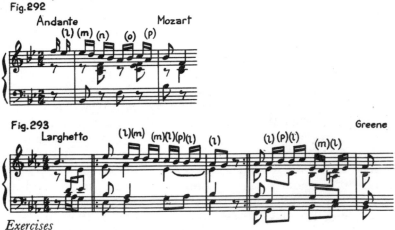

Fig.293

Exercises

1. Write out the foundation chords in Figs. 292 and 293 and add their figuring.

2. Analyse the foundation chords of the following passages and give the function of each note in the melody.

Ex.2

Conclusions

8. At this point we will interrupt our present studies. We have come a long way and you now have a wide vocabulary of chords and other devices to draw upon for your own writing. If you doubt this, remind yourself that the great musicians of the 16th century, including our English madrigal composers, built their reputations on little more than the triads and their inversions, suspensions and passing notes—say, Chapters 10, 11, 14, 15, and 17: and even Haydn and Mozart would find most of their basic material in this volume. So you, too, have plenty of equipment: now you need practice in composing. Get into the habit of putting your ideas down on paper. Be curious about all pieces of music you come across: notice the chords used and the style of the writing: and try to hear in your mind's ear the exact sounds indicated by the ink on the paper. Seeing music goes hand in hand with writing music.

9. Finally, here are some miscellaneous exercises for you to work. They belong to no single chapter but do not go beyond the limits of this volume. Some are for instruments instead of voices: these are simple in style and you should have little difficulty in dealing with them. The name of the composer is given: try to write as he would have written: imitate his method as exactly as you can.

Miscellaneous Exercises

(i) Add a part for tenor:—

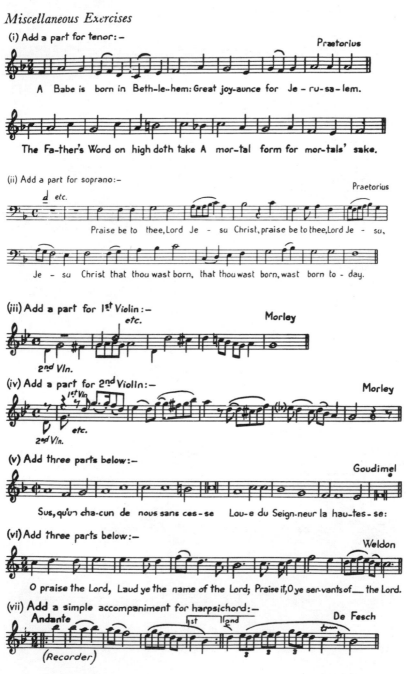

Praetorius

A   Babe is   born in   Beth-le-hem: Great joy-aunce for   Je - ru-sa- lem.

The Fa-ther's Word on   high doth take A   mor-tal   form for   mor-tals' sake.

(ii) Add a part for soprano:—

Praetorius

d etc.

Praise be to   thee, Lord Je - su Christ, praise be to thee, Lord Je - su,

Je - su   Christ that thou wast born,   that thou wast   born, wast   born to - day.

(iii) Add a part for 1st Violin:—

etc.

Morley

2nd Vln.

(iv) Add a part for 2nd Violin:—

Morley

1st Vln.

etc.

2nd Vln.

(v) Add three parts below:—

Goudimel

Sus, qu'un cha-cun de   nous sans ces-se   Lou-e du Seign-neur la hau-tes-se:

(vi) Add three parts below:—

Weldon

O praise the Lord, Laud ye the   name of the Lord; Praise it, O ye ser-vants of ___ the Lord.

(vii) Add a simple accompaniment for harpsichord:—

Andante

De Fesch

1st   2nd

(Recorder)

(viii) Complete the 2ⁿᵈ Violin part:—

(ix) Complete the following for two horns and bassoon:—

(x) Complete the following in three parts:—

(xi) Complete the following in three parts:—

(xii) Add an accompaniment for violin, viola and bass:—

APPENDIX A. MELODY-WRITING

1. Some composers have the gift of being able to write melodies spontaneously. Schubert was one of them: he was specially blessed in this regard. On the other hand, Beethoven was rarely satisfied with his first thoughts on a melody. Melody-writing was, to him, a laborious task. He would shape and re-shape his ideas until the finished passage sometimes bore little resemblance to the original sketches.

2. Many of us lack Schubert's gift and we have not the time (in the examination room) to spend hours or days in following Beethoven's example. We have to call such technique as we possess to our aid and get something down on paper. The following paragraphs are intended as guides in developing this technique.

Foundations of Melody-Writing

3. A melody must have an idea; and it must have design. Both these essentials will be supported by or built upon rhythm and harmony. But rhythm and harmony can produce no result without an idea and a design.

The Melodic Idea

4. The idea may be a small phrase (perhaps only two notes) which strikes the memory through the ear and is recognizable whenever it recurs. There may be more than one idea; but there must be one. It will stand out by reason of its rhythmic or melodic features. If you turn to a song-book and play the tunes listed below you will be able to pick out the salient idea or ideas of each one. Repetitions of the idea may not be exact, but the characteristic features will be recognizable.

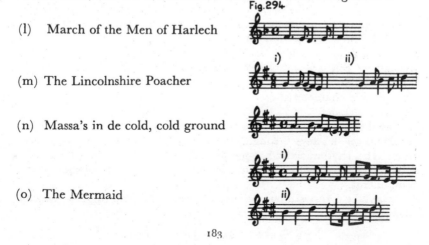

Fig.294

(l)   March of the Men of Harlech

(m)   The Lincolnshire Poacher

(n)   Massa's in de cold, cold ground

(o)   The Mermaid

(p) The Jolly Miller

(q) Pretty Polly Oliver

5. In (l) above, the prominent idea is both melodically and rhythmically striking: we hear it ten times in each verse. In (m), the repeated notes of the first idea stand out clearly: the second idea is less striking but its rise to the highest note in the song gives it importance. In (n), the notes of the main idea are presented in slightly different form and rhythm eleven times in each verse.

Fig.295   Stephen Foster

This melody is simple, yet it is a masterly composition by reason of its telling use of a single series of notes.[1] The tune at (o) has two ideas: the first we hear six times, but you will see that the statements in bars 7 and 9 (and the repetition in the refrain) are more compact than in bars 1 and 2: the whole of bar 1 has been collapsed into a half bar. In (p), the motif of the repeated note is dominant throughout the song. Lastly, the principal idea in (q) does not appear until bar 2, though its rhythm has been stated at the beginning.

6. The idea in a melody is not always so obvious as in the songs referred to. But it is impossible to discover a melody which has stood the test of time, either in folk- or art-music, that has no core, no recognizable characteristics.

Design in Melodies

7. The design of a tune will depend largely on the presentation of the idea, and on the keys through which the tune moves. That is to say, on melodic, rhythmic and harmonic progressions. Music, as we know it, derives much of its interest from the *repetition* and *contrast* of these three components.

8. If we take a very simple phrase of three notes—*doh, ray, me*—we can answer it, equally simply, by *fah, ray, doh*.

[1] See Note on Scales and Modes in Book II.

Here we have an ascending phrase with tonic/dominant harmony contrasted with a descending one which introduces subdominant harmony as well. The contrast is more marked if we vary the rhythm of the answering phrase.

The analysis of this design is phrase L followed by phrase M. It is a simple yet satisfactory piece of music. Still using these two phrases, we can lead M away to the dominant, and then *either* re-introduce the version in Fig. 297, to make L M L M; *or* add a repetition of the rhythm of M before leading back to L—thus producing a design of L M M L.

Next we can build a longer piece shaped L M L M : M M : L M. Here we are more aware of moving from the tonic to secondary triads in bars 5 and 6, so that we welcome the final return of L in the 7th bar. We are also demonstrating the qualities of M in the middle section, before giving the ear the opportunity to recognize the re-appearance of L.

9. This is a skeleton explanation of the principles of design in melody—and in all musical composition. There are many other designs but they, too, are based on three factors: (i) the *statement* of one or more ideas:

(ii) *contrast* in presenting those ideas: and (iii) the *restatement* of all or some of that material. Sometimes there is also (iv) the *discussion* (or, as we say, development) of some of that material (as in Fig. 300).

10. You should analyse some tunes, looking for melodic, rhythmic and harmonic features. If your choice began with 'Men of Harlech', you might find that the design is something as follows:

‖: L   M   L   N :‖ L L LLLL| link M   L   N ‖
F I II-V I-IV cad. in I V I   I   IV-I II-V I-IV cad. in I

You will have noticed the discussion of L in the middle section, and that the last section is very nearly the same as the first.

The Key Sequence

11. We have already mentioned this in Chapter 18, paras. 24–26. A very short or simple song-verse may need no key change. But usually the length will demand some relief from tonic harmony, in which case an excursion can be made to the dominant (or relative major) and further afield still, if desired. Space must be left for the return to the tonic and for its re-establishment.

12. When writing a melody, always carry the prevailing tonality in your head. Otherwise you may find you have arrived in a foreign key with little hope of a safe return. So watch your pivot chords, and be careful that the cadences follow some pattern that we have been using in the main chapters of this volume—such as $VI - V - I$ or $II^7 - V^7 - I$, and so on.

The Rhythmic Plan

13. As we are at the moment concerned with melody-writing, the rhythmic plan will almost wholly depend on the melody itself. But you should remember that (as we found in Chapter 18, para. 10) it is possible to add interest by rhythmic patterns in the underlying parts or accompaniment (para. 21 below).

14. In a melody, a rhythmic pattern repeated too often may create monotony: variation in the rhythm is helpful in ensuring interest. Verdi, in his aria ' La donna è mobile ' (from *Rigoletto*), gives us a square rhythmic design which, only at the last (and the right) moment, is saved from banality by the introduction of a new pattern.

Fig. 301

If you tap this out you will appreciate the importance of the sustained crotchet (*)—the first accented crotchet in the verse—followed by the isolated rhythm of the cadence. But usually it is dangerous to maintain so even a pulse: your audience may not wait for your magical moment at the very end.

15. Mozart (writing in an earlier age) solves the problem of the two-bar phrase rather differently in *The Marriage of Figaro* (' Se vuol ballare ' —'If you are after a little amusement ').

Fig. 302

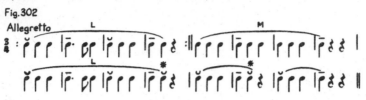

The rhythm of L (repeated) is balanced by the even notes of M. On the return of L, its final crotchet (*) is the cue for a two-bar extension before the cadence. Later in the same opera, at ' Voi che sapete ', Mozart builds his twelve-bar period from an original phrase of four bars comprising both L and M. But we hear L twice more, followed by a two-bar phrase on a free rhythm, before the period is completed by the re-appearance of M.

Fig. 303

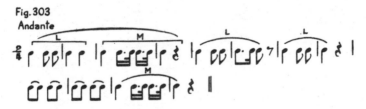

16. The question of rhythm *separated* from any melodic or harmonic line is important. Examine the rhythmic patterns of the songs given in Fig. 294, and any others you have at hand.

17. Setting several verses to one melody may create problems. Exact repetition can become dull; and variations in the word-stresses may make such a course impossible. So watch for opportunities to alter (and often to expand) a phrase on its second or third appearance: this can give new life to an old series of notes. For example, Stanford, at the opening of verses 1 and 2 of ' Devon, O Devon ', writes

Fig. 304

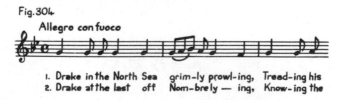

1. Drake in the North Sea   grim-ly prowl-ing,   Tread-ing his
2. Drake at the last   off   Nom-bre ly —   ing,   Know-ing the

But the words of the last verse suggest different treatment and so, using the same notes, he varies the rhythm.

Fig. 305

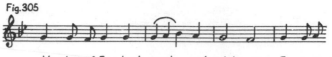

Va - lour of Eng-land gaunt— and white-ning, Far in a

He has expanded the second bar of his original version into two bars. Again, the refrain of the first two verses runs

Fig. 306

De-von, O De-von, in wind and rain!____

But to give greater emphasis to the same phrase in the last verse he adds an extra bar:

Fig. 307

Stanford

De-von, O De-von, in wind _____ and rain!

These are rhythmic subtleties which are not beyond your capacity. But they need thought.

18. The climax of a song often requires a special effect. This can be carried out in a number of ways. The note of climax can be sounded louder (or softer): it may be pitched higher than any other note (Fig. 308): it may be sustained until a suspension forces it downwards (Fig. 309): or, again, it may be held on a pause (as in ' John Peel '). That is, a special moment can be emphasized by intensity, by pitch or by the interruption of the regular flow. The circumstances of each melody must decide which is the most effective method to use for making the climax.

Fig. 308

'Austria'

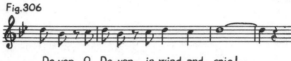

Fig. 309

Moderato con moto

Brahms

How love-ly is— Thy dwell-ing place, O Lord ____ of Hosts, O Lord of Hosts.

The Accompaniment

19. A full discussion of accompaniment is beyond the scope of this volume. But, briefly, it may be said that a true accompaniment should

support the forces it is accompanying and not seek to make itself over-important: lines of sound which have as much interest as the main melody cease to be only accompaniment and become an integral part of the texture. Examples of the first kind are the accompaniment to 'La donna è mobile' (Verdi) and to 'Voi che sapete' (Mozart): of the latter, the 'Prize Song' from *The Mastersingers* (Wagner), 'Devon, O Devon' (Stanford), many of the *lieder* of Schumann and Brahms, and most part-songs for several voices. There are many inter-mediate stages. The choice must depend on the degree of support called for by the melody and the circumstances of the composition.

20. The type of accompaniment also affords a wide choice. Most of our quotations are for voices, but you will see that the accompaniment in Fig. 292 is effective for a simple melody: that in Fig. 233 shows the same pattern slightly modified: in Fig. 86 the accompaniment is closely allied to broken chords: and in Fig. 215 it has a repeated-chord motif: that in Fig. 87 is more complex, comprising two middle parts and an independent bass: and Figs. 83 and 176 show a still more inte-grated texture. There are infinite ways of presenting a melody and giving it harmonic support; and often a mixture of styles is employed, as in Fig. 107.

21. But whatever form the accompaniment may take, it can give the melody more than mere support. It can maintain an underlying rhythm ('The Erl King', Schubert); help to create the atmosphere of the song ('The Trout', Schubert); or (and most important) it can move or mark the rhythm while the melody is stationary ('The Blue Danube', Johann Strauss).

J. Strauss

Fig. 310

22. This seems the right moment to stress the merit of *silence* in a song line. Don't hesitate to let the soloist *rest*, while the accompaniment maintains the progress of the composition—and, sometimes, vice versa. Practise your rests !

Writing it down

23. If you are given a phrase or an idea on which to write a melody (as in an examination) your inspiration will be restricted. First, you must decide which melodic or rhythmic fragment you are going to raise to a state of importance by repetition and discussion. Then, sketch the probable shape of your melody (if you have a choice) and estimate where the chief midway (dominant) cadence will be. After this you

will possibly choose the spot for any free material (free from the main ideas, that is): or, alternatively, you may prefer to develop the main idea (on the lines of ' Men of Harlech '). You will think of the harmonic shape, and the modulations involved. You will look to see if the melodic or rhythmic shape of the midway cadence can be the same (but in a different key) as the final cadence: will it create unity, or give the effect of overmuch repetition? All this time, the pencil is lightly dotting a note here and there—now in the top line, now in the bass—jotting down a figure or drawing a phrase-mark. But nothing is permanent as yet: and it won't be until the pencil sketch is complete and to your liking.

24. If you have a free hand from the start, you can take the first idea that comes into your mind and jot it down. It may be useful, or it may be discarded later. But put it down. Then begin to build round it. Don't try to finish the first bar before turning to the second: both of them may more suitably become bars 3 and 4, or 7 and 8. Sketch in a well-shaped phrase: jot in its bass; then find a companion to balance it. Allow the fertility of your imagination to shape your melody and its accompanying harmonies.

25. Finally, in Fig. 311, on pages 192-4, are notes on the stages (and the thoughts prompting them) by which a melody was actually composed. No attempt has been made to tidy up the result. Every individual has his own way of working: read these notes and see if you can learn anything from them. Study Fig. 311, and then do the following exercises.

Exercises

1. Continue these melodies. Sketch in the supporting harmonies, especially at the cadences.

(v) Tempo di Valse

(vi) Grave

(vii) Allegro

(viii) Vivace

etc.

2. Compose melodies to which the following are the melodic climaxes. Sketch in the harmonies.

Ex.2

(i) Andante

(ii) Moderato

(iii) Allegro

(iv) Andante espressivo

(v) Allegro

(vi) Adagio

(vii) Andante

(viii) Allegro

1. The first thought.

2. The first thought extended, with some harmonies dotted in. The pitch is too low. Lift it up and give it the freedom of violin writing—as in 3.

3. Better. But it does not feel like a *first* phrase. Is there an opening phrase to which this can be the sequel?

4. The time and mood are fixed. A first phrase is added. The second is modified at the half-close.

5. Now a short development of the rhythm of the first three notes of 1. This can conveniently lead back to 3 as the final section (if the cadence is altered to the tonic).

6. While writing this out, the idea occurs of repeating phrase 'A' in another part—to extend this section. It is sketched in at 7, with some suspensions in the solo part.

7. The solo is now too low. An arpeggio can lift it for the final cadence (see 3). But the arpeggio is so striking that it can hardly stand by itself: —hence the alteration to the second bar.

9. A more finished copy is given overleaf.

Fig.311 APPENDIX A. MELODY-WRITING 193

I I⁶ IV I⁶

3. *(Violin)*

9.

Violin

Piano

APPENDIX B
Conventions in writing Music Manuscript

1. Although all composers, including students, are encouraged to write what they like, the method by which they put their ideas on paper should conform to common practice so that performers and those who see the manuscript can understand readily what is written.

Take a pride in your musical calligraphy: don't strain the patience of those who have to read your work.

Notice how printed music is set out on the page: don't scorn to learn from the very beautiful printing produced by most music publishers today.

Space each bar well: don't cram the notes together.

In vocal music, the placing of the notes should be governed by the space taken by the *legible* writing of the words: don't squash the words together.

Leave room for marks of expression, especially crescendo and decrescendo signs (━━━━━━ ━━━━━━): and put in phrase-marks or (in string music) bowing-marks.

Give particular attention to the first line of a work: bracket the requisite number of staves; write in the clef-signs, key-signature and time-signature; write the names of the instruments or voices concerned to the left of the bracket; and make a note of the *tempo* of the work above the top stave.

The time-signature is not repeated at the beginning of each subsequent line: the original signature remains in force unless and until the time is changed.

If a change of time- and/or key-signature coincides with the beginning of a line, the new signature is also written at the end of the previous line. (This is important.)

In writing for

piano; bracket the two staves together.

organ; bracket three staves, with an extra one to join the two manual staves.

piano and one voice (or instrument); bracket three staves, with an extra one to join the two piano staves.

voices; bracket as many staves as are required.

orchestra; bracket the complete set of staves, and add additional brackets for the woodwind, brass, chorus (if any), piano (if any), and strings.

In manuscript, bar-lines are usually ruled continuously through the staves of each group of instruments. In vocal music it is better to rule the bar-lines on the staves only: this leaves plenty of space for underlaying the words.

The final bar is usually shortened by the number of beats (or half-beats) which precede the first complete bar of all.

Fig. 313

Set down the notes in each bar in such a manner as to make clear the prevailing time (simple triple, compound duple, etc.). Take care to distinguish between $\frac{3}{4}$ and $\frac{6}{8}$; and between $\frac{3}{2}$ and $\frac{6}{4}$ (see Fig. 75).

Underlaying is the apportioning of syllables to notes, as in a song or choral work. When two or more notes are allotted to one syllable they should be slurred. In addition, quavers and semi-quavers are either bracketed in beat- or half-bar-groups (as in fig. 314); or they are grouped according to the syllables of the text—if there are two or more notes to a syllable they are joined together, otherwise they are separated (see ex. 7 on p. 125). Multi-syllable words are divided as when hyphenated: a syllable is set down complete and is not spelled out letter by letter.

Fig. 314   Stanford

Metrical irregularities—duplets, triplets, etc.—are discussed in Chapter 8, paras. 20 and 21.

The ornaments you are most likely to come across are set out in Figs. 180, 214 and 217. For further study of this subject, you should read the specialized articles in a musical dictionary or text-book.

2. Signs:

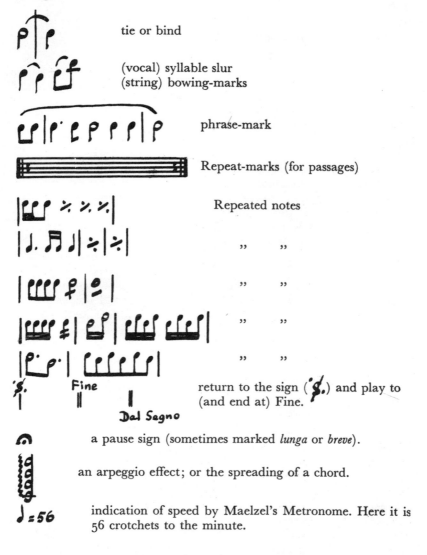

tie or bind

(vocal) syllable slur
(string) bowing-marks

phrase-mark

Repeat-marks (for passages)

Repeated notes

     ,,   ,,

     ,,   ,,

     ,,   ,,

     ,,   ,,

return to the sign (𝄋) and play to
(and end at) Fine.

a pause sign (sometimes marked *lunga* or *breve*).

an arpeggio effect; or the spreading of a chord.

indication of speed by Maelzel's Metronome. Here it is
56 crotchets to the minute.

8va. or 8. . . . . . .   Play the notes an octave higher.
8va. bassa or 8va. sotta   Play the notes an octave lower.

V up bow   } in string writing: toe } in organ writing.
Ⴖ down bow }   heel }

o

3. Musical terms in common use:

SPEED:

Adagio	slow	langsam
Allegretto	fairly quick, less quick than *allegro*	
Allegro	brisk, quick	schnell
Andante	with moderate movement	gehend
Andantino	a little quicker than *andante*	
Grave	very slow and solemn	schwer
Largo	slow and broad	breit
Lento	slow	sehr langsam
Presto	fast	sehr schnell
Accel(erando)	get faster	beschleunigend
Allarg(ando)	broaden	breiter werdend
Con moto	with movement	bewegt
L'istesso tempo	in the same time	
Meno mosso	less movement (i.e., slower)	weniger bewegt
Più mosso	more movement (i.e., faster)	etwas bewegter
Rall(entando) } *Rit(ardando)*	gradually becoming slower	langsamer werdend zögernd
Rit(enuto)	(the speed) held back	zurückgehalten
Stringendo	hurrying on	beschleunigend
Tempo primo (*a tempo*)	in the original time	voriges Zeitmass

EXPRESSION:

Animato	with life, animated	lebhaft
Con anima	with feeling, soul	beseelt
Con brio	with vigour, spirit	feurig
Cantabile } *Cantando*	'singingly'	gesangvoll
Dolce	sweetly	weich
Espressivo	expressive	ausdrucksvoll
Giusto	strict, exact (time)	
Grazioso	graceful	anmutig
Legato	smoothly, slurred	gebunden
Leggiero	light	
Marcato	accented	
Maestoso	stately	feierlich
Pesante	heavily	gewichtig
Scherzando	playfully, jokingly	
Sost(enuto)	sustained	
Stacc(ato)	detached	gestossen
Vivace	lively, vivacious	lebhaft
p piano	soft	
pp pianissimo	very soft	
mp mezzo piano	fairly soft	

mf mezzo forte	fairly loud
f forte	loud
ff fortissimo	very loud
sfz sforzando	forced
sfp sforzato-piano	accented, then soft
cresc(endo)	growing louder
dim(inuendo) } *decresc(endo)*	growing softer

GENERAL:

Arco	with the bow	mit Bogen
Assai	very	sehr
Attacca	straight on, play on at once	
Doppio	double	
Da Capo (al Fine)	from the beginning (to the *Fine* mark)	
m.d. Mano destra	right hand	
m.s. Mano sinistra	left hand	
Meno	less	
Molto	much	
Più	more	
Pizz(icato)	plucked	
Poch(etto)	very little	
Poco	a little, rather	
Quasi	giving the effect of	gleichsam
Secco	short	
Segue	follows	
Sempre	always	
Senza (Sordino)	without (mute)	ohne (Dämpfer)
Simile	similar	
Subito	suddenly	
Con Sordino	with mute	mit Dämpfer
Ten(uto)	held, sustained	gehalten
Troppo	too much	
Tutti	all, everyone	
Una corda	use one string only (of piano), i.e., soft pedal	
V.S. Volti subito	turn over quickly	

INDEX OF QUOTATIONS

ANONYMOUS
52 'Alas departynge is ground of woo' (1st half 15th century)
* BACH, J. S.
45 (Prelude and) Fugue in E, Bk. II, '48'
61 (Toccata and) Fugue in D minor for organ (final bars)
90 Suite in B minor for solo violin (Allemande, Double)
102 (Fantasia and) Fugue in C minor for organ
104 Mass in B minor,
   (i) 'Gloria in excelsis Deo'
   (ii) 'Gratias agimus'
   (iii) 'Qui tollis'
106 Chorale, 'Ein' feste Burg'
116 Mass in B minor, 'Et expecto'
166 Partita No. 2 in C minor (Rondeau)
174 Chorale, St. John Passion, No. 27
190 Chorale, 'Nun freut euch'
201 Trio Sonata No. 3 in D minor for organ (Adagio)
224 (i) 2-part Invention in F
   (ii) 2-part Invention in D minor
   (iii) The Anna Magdalena Book
234 (i) Chorale, 'Meines Lebens letzte Zeit'
   (ii) Chorale, 'Ich dank' dir, Gott'
252 French Suite in B minor (Minuet)
254 French Suite in E flat (Gavotte)
255 2-part Invention in C
283 (i) Chorale, 'Nun danket'
   (ii) Chorale, 'O Gott, du frommer Gott'
   (iii) Chorale, 'Herzliebster Jesu, was hast du'
287 Chorale, St. Matthew Passion No. 49
Chap. 22 Ex. 2 (ii) Suite in B minor (Overture)
BEETHOVEN
48 Symphony No. 7 in A (Allegretto, final bars)
49 Symphony No. 7 in A (Allegretto, beginning)
50 Symphony No. 3 in E flat (Trio)
56 Piano Sonata in C minor, op. 13 (Finale, final bars)
80 Symphony No. 9 in D minor (Scherzo)
83 Piano Concerto No. 5, 'Emperor' (Adagio)

86 Piano Sonata in G, op. 79 (Andante)
89 Piano Sonata in A flat, op. 26 (Finale)
96 String Quartet in F, op. 59 No. 1 (beginning)
178 Minuet in G
BERG, ALBAN
92 Wozzeck, Act 1, bar 134
BLOW, JOHN
172 Anthem, 'Behold, O God our defender'
BRAHMS, J.
87 Symphony No. 4 in E minor (Andante)
97 Requiem, 'How lovely is thy dwelling place'
231 The St. Anthony Variations
309 Requiem
BYRD, WILLIAM
64 Responses
189 Short Service (Venite)
CHOPIN
13 Nocturne in G major, op. 37 No. 2
15 Nocturne in E flat, op. 9 No. 2
DEBUSSY
19 Prélude à l'après-midi d'un faune
DE FESCH
Chap. 22 Misc. Ex. (vii) Recorder Sonata in B flat
DVORAK
284 Symphony, 'From the New World' (Largo)
FOSTER, STEPHEN
295 'Massa's in de cold, cold ground'
GIBBONS, ORLANDO
163 Song 4. The Song of Hannah
230 Madrigal, 'The Silver Swan'
264 Madrigal, 'The Silver Swan'
GOUDIMEL, C.
Chap. 22 Misc. Ex. (v) Psalter of 1565, Psalm CV
GREENE, MAURICE
293 'O God of my righteousness'
HANDEL
29 Harpsichord Suite in G minor (Gigue)
69 Samson, 'Then round about the starry throne'
91 'Droop not young lover'
101 Messiah, 'The people that walked in darkness'
103 Messiah, recit, 'And the angel said unto them'
111 Messiah, 'Hallelujah' Chorus

* The German title is given to Chorales if there are difficulties in identification.

HANDEL—Contd.
115 *Messiah*, 'All we like sheep' (final section)
154 *Messiah*, 'Rejoice greatly'
182 The Water Music (Air)
Chap. 13, Ex. 7 Anthem, 'Zadok the Priest'
291 'Where e'er you walk'
Chap. 22 Ex. 2 (iv) Harpsichord Suite in G minor
HAYDN, J.
66 *Creation*, 'The heavens are telling'
99 String Quartet in D, op. 64 No. 5 ('The Lark') (beginning)
277 Missa, 'St. Theresa' (Sanctus)
Chap. 22 Ex. 2 (iii) Sonata in C (Adagio)
308 'Austria'
HOLST, G.
28 *The Planets*, Mercury (Figure II)
HUMPERDINCK
232 *Hansel and Gretel*, Overture
HUMPHREY, PELHAM
63 Anglican Chant in C (associated with the Anthems for Easter Day)
HYMN TUNES
94 'York'
148 (i) 'Hanover'
149 'Psalm 68'
158 'Tallis's Canon'
308 'Austria'
LASSO, ORLANDO di
62 Missa, Quinti Toni (Agnus Dei)
MENDELSSOHN
85 Symphony No. 4 in A ('Italian') (first movement)
290 Symphony No. 3 in A minor ('Scottish') (Scherzo)
MORLEY, THOMAS
164 Canzonet, 'Miraculous love's wounding'
165 Canzonet, 'I go before my darling'
167 Canzonet, 'Go ye, my canzonets'
200 Canzonet, 'I should for grief and anguish'
Chap. 22 Misc. Ex. (iii) Two-part Canzonets ('The Catherine Wheel')
Chap. 22 Misc. Ex. (iv) Two-part Canzonets ('The Sad One')
MOZART
65 String Quartet in D, K. 575 (Minuet)
68 Allegro for piano, K. 3
107 Clarinet Quintet, K. 581 (beginning)
143 *Cosi fan tutte*, Quintet in Act I
177 Violin Sonata in B flat, K.8
Chap. 13 Ex. 7 *Cosi fan tutte*, Trio in Act I

195 Piano Sonata in C minor, K. 457 (Finale)
215 Piano Sonata in A minor, K. 310 (beginning)
221 Piano Sonata in B flat, K. 333 (Finale)
Chap. 16 Ex. 1 *Cosi fan tutte*, Act II 'Ah lo veggio'
Chap. 17 Ex. 4 (iii) Minuet, K.2 (iv) Minuet, K.5
280 Horn Concerto in E flat, K. 495
292 *Cosi fan tutte*, Duet in Act II,
Chap. 22 Ex. 2 (i) Rondo for piano, K. 494
Chap. 22 Misc. Ex. (viii) Divertimento in D, K. 131 (Finale)
Chap. 22 Misc. Ex. (ix) Divertimento in D, K. 205 (Trio)
Chap. 22 Misc. Ex. (x) German Dances, K. 509
Chap. 22 Misc. Ex. (xi) German Dances, K. 567
NATIONAL SONGS
11 'Charlie is my darling'
81 'Marching through Georgia'
82 'O where, and O where, is my hieland laddie gone?'
PALESTRINA
150 Missa, Papae Marcelli (Credo)
198 Magnificat (4th Mode)
PALUSELLI, S.
Chap. 22 Misc. Ex. (xii) Divertimento
PHILIPS, PETER
269 Motet, 'Ascendit Deus'
282 Motet, 'Ascendit Deus'
PLAINSONG
32 *Musica Enchiriadis*
PRAETORIUS
114 Carol, 'A rose breaks into bloom' ('Es ist ein Ros' ')
Chap. 22 Misc. Ex. (i) Magnificat, Ecce Maria
Chap. 22 Misc. Ex. (ii) Musae Sionae
PURCELL, HENRY
84 *Dido and Aeneas*, 'To the hills and the vales'
112 Anthem, 'My heart is inditing'
113 *The Fairy Queen*, Entrance of Night
176 *The Fairy Queen*, Rondeau Minuet
286 *The Fairy Queen*, 'Hark! the ech'ing air'
288 *Dido and Aeneas*, Echo chorus
SCHUBERT
175 String Quintet in C (1st movement)
233 String Quintet in C (Finale)

SCHUMANN
216   *Papillons*, No. 11
276   (i) Album for the Young,
          Melody
       (ii) Album for the Young,
          Round
STANFORD, C. V.
304/ Songs of the Sea, 'Devon, O
307   Devon'
314   Songs of the Fleet, 'Sailing at
       Dawn'
STRAUSS, JOHANN
310   *The Blue Danube*
TALLIS, THOMAS
158   Hymn Tune, 'Tallis's Canon'
TOMKINS, THOMAS
199   Madrigal, 'When David heard'
TSCHAIKOVSKY
108   Symphony in B minor ('Pathetic'),
       op. 74 (first movement)
VAUGHAN WILLIAMS, RALPH
77   *Job*, Scene IV, Job's dream

171   Five English Folksongs, 'Just as
       the tide was flowing'
WAGNER
30   *The Mastersingers*, Act II, Sc. 5
       (Beckmesser's Serenade)
70   *The Mastersingers*, Prelude to
       Act III
78   *The Valkyrie*, The Ride of the
       Valkyries
118   *The Mastersingers*, Prelude to
       Act III
139   *Parsifal*, 'The Grail' theme
278   *The Mastersingers*, Prelude
WELDON, JOHN
    Chap. 22 Misc. Ex. (vi) Anthem, 'O
    Praise the Lord'
WALTON, WILLIAM
98   *Belshazzar's Feast* (17 bars after
       Figure 8)
WILBYE, JOHN
47   Madrigal, 'Weep, O mine eyes'

INDEX

(References in brackets are to Book II)

Acciaccatura, 126
Accent, 46–49
Accidental, 12
Accompaniment, 188–9
Additional harmony notes, 68, 103
Anticipation notes, 177–9
Appoggiatura, 127–30
Augmented Intervals, 17
   Sixths (Ch. 29)
   Triad, 23, 135
Auxiliary notes, 100–2
Auxiliary Six-four, 135–6
Cadences, Ch. 7 (Note)
   Authentic, 38–39, 69–70
   Approach to, 37–38, 78, 83
   Half-close, 39–40, 70
   Imperfect, 39–40, 70
   Interrupted, 41, 77–78
   Inverted, 84
   Perfect, 38–39
   Phrygian, (Note on Cadences)
   Plagal, 38–39, 70
Cadential Six-four, 28, 128, 133-5
Cadenza, 135
Changing notes, (Ch. 31)
Chorales, Harmonization of (Ch. 35)
Chord of the Sixth (see Six-three Chords)
Chromatic, Definition, 12–13
   Scale, Ch. 3
   Harmony (Ch. 27)
Clefs, Ch. 2
Close position, 24
Common Chord, 23
Compound Intervals, 18
   Time, 44
Concord, 19–20
Consecutive Intervals, 63 (Note)
   Fifths, 64–65, 177
   Fourths, 65
   Hidden, 66–67
   Octaves, 64
   Seconds, 66, 177
   Sevenths, 66 (Ch. 23)
   (Unisons), 63–64
Counterpoint, 89
Crossing of parts, 61–63
Cycle of Keys, 6–7, 34–35
Decoration in part-writing (Ch. 31)
Degrees of scale, 3–4
Diatonic (definition), 11
Diminished, Intervals, 17
   Sevenths (Ch. 24)
   Triads, 23, 159
Discord, 19–20

Dominant (of scale), 3
Dominant Eleventh (Ch. 25)
   Ninth (Ch. 24)
   Seventh, 158–60, 168–71
   Thirteenth (Ch. 26)
Doubling, 60
Enharmonic, 7
Essential notes, 96
Extended position, 24
False Relation, 164 (Note on Cadences)
Fifths, Consecutive, 64–65, 177
Figured Bass, 18, 25 (Note)
Forbidden consecutives, 63 (Note)
Fourths, 20–21
   Consecutive, 65-66
Harmonic Intervals, 16
   Minor Scale, 32
   Rhythm (Ch. 32)
Hexachord, 8–9
Hidden Consecutives, 66–67
Imitation, 93–94
Implied Harmony, 90
Intervals, Ch. 4
   Augmented, 17
   Chromatic, 16
   Compound, 18
   Diatonic, 16
   Diminished, 17
   Harmonic, 16
   Inversion of, 19
   Major, 17
   Melodic, 16
   Minor, 17
   Perfect, 17
Key Establishment, 84, 148
   Relationship, 34, 144
   Sequence, 148–9, 186
   Signatures, 7, 34
Key Cycle
   Major, 6–7
   Major and Minor, 34–35
Leading note, 3, 67
   Triad on, 24, 67, 81, 107, 170–1
Major Scale, Ch. 1
Major Triads, Chs. 10 and 11
Mediant Triad, 78
Minor Scales, Ch. 6
   Harmonic, 32
   Melodic, 33
Melody Writing, Appendix A
Minor Triads, Ch. 14
Modulation, Chs. 18 and 19, p. 164
Motion
   Conjunct, 54

Motion—*contd.*
  Contrary, 54
  Disjunct, 54
  Oblique, 54
  Similar, 54
Musica ficta, 32
Musical terms, 200–1
Neapolitan Sixth (Ch. 28)
Note-values, 43-44
Octaves, Consecutive, 64
Open Score, 11
Ornaments, 102
Ornamental Resolutions, 121–3
Overlapping, 60–61
Passing notes, Accented (Ch. 31)
  Unaccented, 96–98
Passing Six–four, 136–7, 174
Pedal-points, 39 (Ch. 31)
Pianoforte Keyboard, 4
  Writing for (Appendix D)
Picardy Third, 110
Primary Triads, 24, 67–69
Relative Major and Minor, 34–36
Related Keys, 144
Remote Keys, 144
Rests, 43–44, 189
Retardation, 118
Rhythm, 142, 186–8 (Ch. 32)
Root progressions, 74–78, 148–9
Scales, Chs. 1, 3, 6
Seconds, consecutive, 66, 177
Secondary Sevenths (Ch. 23)
  Triads, 24, 74

Second Inversion of Triads, 27–29, Ch.
  17
Sevenths, Consecutive, 66 (Ch. 23 para.
  7)
  Dominant (see Dominant Seventh)
Short Score, 10
Signs, 199
Simple Time, 44
Six-four Chords, 27–29, Ch. 17
Six-three Chords, 26–27, Chs. 11 and 14
Spacing, 24, 58–60
Strings, Writing for (Appendix C)
Subsidiary Harmony notes, 68, 103
Supertonic Seventh, 161–3, 173–6
Suspensions, Ch. 15 (Ch. 30)
Tetrachords, 5, 31
Tierce de Picardie, 110
Time-signatures, 44–45 (Note)
Tonality, 3
Tonic, 3
Transient Modulations, 148
Triads, Ch. 5
  Inversions, Chs. 11, 14, 17
  Primary, 67–69
  Root positions, Chs. 10, 14
  Secondary, 74
Unessential Notes, 96
Unison, 16
Unrelated Keys, 144
Voice Parts, 54–57
Voice Ranges, 58